FULL CIRCLE

A PROPOSAL TO THE CHURCH
FOR AN ARTS MINISTRY

BY NENA BRYANS

Schuyler Institute for Worship and the Arts
San Carlos, California

Printed in the United States of America.

ISBN 0-944230-00-8
Library of Congress Catalog Card Number 87-62736

Published by
Schuyler Institute for Worship and the Arts
2757 Melendy Drive, Suite 15
San Carlos, California 94070

Sole Selling Agent:
Thomas House Publications

Cover Illustration: Nancy Chinn
Book Design: Phil Porter/Porter Maremaa Design/Berkeley

TABLE OF CONTENTS

FROM THE PUBLISHER

It is a distinct pleasure for Schuyler Institute for Worship and the Arts to participate with Nena Bryans in this publication. *Full Circle* will elicit from the reader feelings of identity with much of what is written here; not only Nena Bryans' thinking, but also that of many important artists, philosophers, teachers, and theologians of the past and present. This book will challenge you to read further, and to look at your own response to arts in the church.

The format of the book is such that your eye will be drawn back and forth from the text to margin quotes. The quotes often enhance or enlarge upon the proximate text. Our hope is that the reader will take time for reflection on his/her personal relationship to the thoughts expressed by the body of text and the marginalia.

Schuyler Institute for Worship and the Arts looks forward to the time when all arts and artists will be fully part of the worship life of churches in all denominations. Finally, we hope that this book will encourage the reader to move toward an arts ministry in the church either directly or indirectly involving the entire congregation in the process of artistic creation and relating that to the process of faith and worship.

Cortlandt S. Bender
President/Founder
Schuyler Institute for Worship and the Arts

PREFACE

I remember my astonishment when a routine mail delivery brought the first draft of *Full Circle* to my desk. Its author, little known to me at the time, asked for a judgement. My response was swift: Publish. Laity and clergy need this. My faculty colleagues concurred.

Later I suspected that the effort sustaining Nena's inquiry was born of probing and persistent questions. Why is productive activity between the arts community and the religious community so infrequent? Is church leadership indifferent, are artists disinterested, or congregations ignorant of the connections? Must much ecclesiastical space by necessity be an assault to the senses? Where are the arts in theological education? Her search yielded no justification for the ambivalence and ambiguity. Rather, it produced a work gathered through a wide-angle lens asking for the churches' authentic recovery of the arts, a recovery based on acceptance of their autonomy and their undeniable role as a primary source.

Full Circle pleads the case for the reuniting of these two errant siblings with compelling testimony reinforced by a practical guide. Theology which ignores the arts, and art which functions as ornament, truncates the capacity of both.

Catherine A. Kapikian
Artist-in-Residence and Director
of the Wesley Theological Seminary
Center for the Arts and Religion

FOREWORD

The term "art ministry" was first suggested to me by Ann Du-
bois of the Presbyterian Vocation Agency when I was sharing
informally with her several years ago my frustration with trying to
deal with the claims on my time and interests between Christian
Education, in which I was formally trained and served many
years, and my own "art form" – sculpture, which gave me much
joy. She responded that perhaps the two might come together
some day in an "Art Ministry." Some time later Margaret Thomp-
son, S.S.J., showed me a pamphlet with the bold letters –
"ART MINISTRY" – the first time I had seen the two words "in
print." This booklet described a religious-women-artists net-
work of Catholic sisters devoted to promoting "a valid and vigor-
ous Art Ministry in the Church."

Still later I attended a conference at Kirkridge, Pennsylvania,
led by Matthew Fox, who opened up the whole theological dimension for the church's concern for the arts. I remember tim-
idly asking him at the end of a session just how the arts and
faith could be more related. He looked at me as though I had
asked him to explain the universe in one sentence. His com-
ment was simply, "So much! Oh, so much!"

So I have wanted to spell out for myself what the "so much"
was, and it has led me into some fascinating reading and con-
versations with many creative people. I cannot begin to give
credit to all those who have encouraged and challenged me
along the way. Yet I must say a special "Thank you" to Catherine Kapikian, Director of the Center for the Arts and Religion at
Wesley Theological Seminary in Washington, D. C., who has
brought together, in her work and her life, so much of the synthesis between faith and art.

Nena Bryans

CHAPTER 1
KINSHIP AND ESTRANGEMENT

Art and religion have been in various relationships throughout human history. They have nourished one another. At times they have been in conflict and often they have been jealous rivals. They are like "close siblings"[1] who bear a strong family resemblance.

The family resemblance is strongest in their similarity of purpose. Religion and art seek to do the same thing. Each begins with a vision and both are preoccupied with representing the vision, giving it form and shape so that others can see and evaluate their vision. The distinction lies in the media and the material. The artist uses clay, paint, poetry, music, and movement. The theologian uses stories, doctrines, liturgies, and ethics.[2]

Not only do their goals spring from the same source, but religion and art have always recognized their need for one another. There seems to be an intimate and necessary relationship for each to do what it seeks to do.

Rabbi Abraham Joshua Heschel, in his book *Quest for God* writes of this:

> What would art have been without the religious sense of mystery and sovereignty, and how dreary would have been religion without the heroic venture of the artist to embody the mysterious in visible forms...The right hand of the artist withers when he forgets the sovereignty of God, and the heart of the religious man has often become dreary without the daring skill of the artist.[3]

And yet, for the past several hundred years, these two siblings

Both art and religion seek mystic experience. Each is the result of an immersion in life. The artist and believer go into the wilderness of the unexplored life and bring from it the fruit of their encounter.

Anthony Padovano

Religion and art have been wed from earliest times. Much of the world's most profound literature has been an attempt to put in words an understanding of the divine. Much of its most creative sculpture and painting has been an effort to capture a religious insight in tangible form.

James Tanis

> *It is my opinion that art lost its basic creative drive the moment it was separated from worship. It severed an umbilical cord and now lives its own sterile life, generating and degenerating itself.*
>
> **Ingmar Bergman**

> *Without monsters and gods, art cannot enact our drama ...when they were abandoned as untenable superstitions, art sank into melancholy. It became fond of the dark, and enveloped its objects in the nostalgic intimations of a half-lit world.*
>
> **Mark Rothko**

have lived in relative isolation from one another. The reason for this separation is complex. During the Middle Ages and most of the Renaissance, western art was primarily Christian, both in content and style. Almost all of the artistic energy was channeled into religious themes and concerns. With the onset of the age of reason, the advent of literacy, and the forces inherent in the Protestant Reformation, things began to change. Artists wanted to be free of the restraints of the church and began to move into other areas of interest. Art became secularized, a means of bringing beauty into life rather than being in service to the church. At the same time, the church, for the most part, turned its back on the artists, and rid itself of images and the visual arts. By the 18th century the separation was all but complete and the estrangement has lasted to the present day.[4] Though we want to focus primarily on the effect of this estrangement on religion, you will see on this page the comments of two artists on the estrangement's effect on the arts.

Both the Bergman and Rothko insights at the left describe a contemporary art that has become trivial, commercial, and elitist, cut off from the more profound depths of meaning. It is the effect of this isolation on religion that we wish to explore in some detail. Martin Marty, noted interpreter of our contemporary religious scene, states that our thinking reflects a "sense of exhaustion" because it has been over-loaded. We live with a dangerously one-sided way of viewing the world. Our culture, devoted almost entirely to learning technical skills, has left us with a "vacuum of the heart."[5] We wish to show that a greater openness to the arts and all they offer will help to balance our way of living in the world. We wish to suggest that it is vital to both religion and the arts that the alienation that has existed between them be overcome.

Theologian John Westerhoff, Professor at Duke University School of Divinity, asks the question, "What has Zion to do with Bohemia?" – or, in essence, what has the religious life to do with the artistic life? His answer is "Everything!" and he goes on to say that "human individual and corporate life is at stake in the estrangement of Zion and Bohemia. Their reunion may well be the greatest challenge facing religious education in our day."[6]

The purpose of this volume is to acknowledge the unhealthy separation that has existed between art and religion, to point to encouraging signs of change, and to suggest ways to further the reconciliation of these siblings.

We attest to the idea that art and religion must not stand in isolation from one another. If religion refuses to recognize the revelatory power of art, the museum eclipses the prophetic function of the temple and the catalogue replaces the bulletin as a guide to the liturgy. As religion addresses the imminent and transcendent dimension of life and art provides the material place for the indwelling of the numinous, both articulate in symbolic language all that it means to be human. Art and religion must yield their insights in concert with one another.

Catherine Kapikian

Religion without artistic images is qualitatively impoverished, art without religion is in danger of triviality, superficiality, or subservience to commercial or political interests.

Margaret Miles

CHAPTER 2
NEW SPIRITUALITY IN THE ARTS

As a backdrop to our considerations, we must note the unprecedented explosion of interest in the arts in our society today. Attendance at art museums is phenomenal. As an illustration, more than 10,000 people crowded into the Philadelphia Museum of Art on a hot Sunday in August, 1986, to see the work of Diego Rivera on the closing day of the exhibit. There is a frenzy of building new art museums. [7] Musical concerts, the theatre, and dance programs draw increasing numbers. At the same time, church membership and attendance is down.

Why do the arts play such an important role in our culture today? Jacques Barzun, in his Mellon Lectures in the Fine Arts in 1973, stated that "art...has become a gateway to the realm of the spirit for all those over whom old religions have lost their hold." [8] Art has given a new home to the "desires which failing religions left floating." [9] Even the places where the art is housed take on added meaning.

Whether or not we are willing to concede that as architect Arata Isozaki says, "the gods are no more," we have to acknowledge that for many people the arts provide an encounter with a transcendent dimension. Even a voice from within the church, Paul Tillich, has written in his book *Theology of Culture*, "the new religious feeling of our time comes through art rather than through the churches." [10]

An article in the *New York Times* (November 11, 1979) entitled "Signs of a New Spirituality in the Arts," pointed out that "a good many artists are sharing with organized religion an unembarrassed interest in a non-material world." Artists are delving into questions originally posed by religion, both in their work and the explanation of their work. In 1977-78 Jane and John

Dillenberger, long-time pioneers in bringing faith and art together, assembled an exhibition of work by contemporary artists entitled "Perceptions of the Spirit." [11] They sought to illustrate how central were spiritual perceptions to many of the major artists of this century.

The retrospective of modern art held at the Hirshhorn Museum in Washington, D.C., in the fall of 1984, had as its theme "Content: a Contemporary Focus 1974-1984." In the program notes the following comments were made:

> Metaphysical ideas, social commentary, and use of illusion and metaphor – elements that many artists and critics had considered inappropriate to art only ten years ago – are now essential to the creation and understanding of much contemporary art. Content, in a word, has emerged as a central issue of the international avant-garde.

> ...During the last ten years, works of art with psychological, spiritual, and metaphysical content have appeared in significant numbers for the first time since the heyday of surrealism in the 1930s...Religious imagery, ritual action, and monumental themes of immortality and the soul have reemerged as central ideas...

> ...During the last ten years, artists have consciously expanded the scope of their art to include the concerns of the world in which we live. The issues of our time have become both inspiration and reason for the creation of art in the post-Modern era.

The inaugural exhibit of the Robert O. Anderson building of the Los Angeles County Museum in November, 1986, was entitled "The Spiritual in Art," taking its name from Wassily Kandin-

The function of the artist is to make the spiritual so that it is there to be possessed.

Robert Motherwell

It is very important for the artist to gauge his position aright, to realize that he has a duty to himself, that he is not king of the castle but rather a servant of a nobler purpose. He must search deeply into his own soul, develop and tend it, so that his art has something to clothe, and does not remain a glove without a hand.
The artist must have something to say...

Wassily Kandinsky

The art of today embodies the spiritual nurtured to the point of revelation.

Wassily Kandinsky

It is the artist's mission to penetrate as far as may be toward that secret ground where primal law feeds growth...Our beating heart drives us downward, far down to the primal ground...My hand is entirely the instrument of a more distant sphere nor is it my head that functions in my work; it is something else.

Paul Klee

When religion, science and morality are shaken...and when the outer supports threaten to fall, man turns his gaze from externals in on to himself. Literature, music and art are the first and most sensitive spheres in which this spiritual revolution makes itself felt.

Wassily Kandinsky

sky's seminal book of the same name. Mircea Eliade treats the same issues in his article "The Sacred and the Modern Artist" stating that "the great majority of artists do not seem to have 'faith' in the traditional sense of the word. They are not consciously 'religious.' Nonetheless, we maintain that the sacred...is present in their work." [12]

Artists themselves often give verbal expression to the intent and deeper meaning of the work they do. M. C. Escher wrote that he felt ripen in himself a conscious wish to use his imaginary images to approach infinity as purely and as closely as possible. What he sought to portray, he said, was "deep, deep infinity!" [13]

Because artists often play a balancing role in the society in which they live, we can agree with Erich Neumann that the art of our time displays a "radical spiritualism" [14] in order to compensate for the outward materialism which dominates our culture.

CHAPTER 3
CHANGING ATTITUDES IN THE CHURCH

Having looked at some of the significant changes in the art world over the last generation, let us turn our attention to the churches to see what attitudes are present there. More than thirty-five years ago, Dorothy Sayers wrote:

> In such things as politics, finance, sociology, and so on, there really is a philosophy and a Christian tradition...
>
> *But oddly enough, we have no Christian aesthetic – no Christian philosophy of the Arts.* The Church as a body has never made up her mind about the Arts...She has, of course, from time to time puritanically denounced the Arts as irreligious and mischievous, or tried to exploit the Arts as a means to the teaching of religion and morals...And there have, of course, been plenty of writers on aesthetics who happened to be Christians, but they seldom made any consistent attempt to relate their aesthetic to the central Christian dogmas. [15]

Since her writing there have been many who have explored the relationship between faith and the arts.

One of the early voices was Walter Nathan, whose book, *Art and the Message of the Church*, was published in 1961 by Westminster Press. Nathan dealt with the spiritual foundation of the arts and provided a most helpful review of our heritage in the arts. He explored the function of Christian art as well as its scope and limits. In the final chapter Nathan challenged the church with some very forward-looking suggestions. He called on seminaries to give leadership.

Since what is primarily required at this stage is informed leadership, we must look to the divinity schools to provide it...Once the theological schools accept their responsibility for the training of the younger generation in the field of art, we can expect to get the informed leadership that is now largely unavailable. In the meantime, church workers and pastors are left to their own initiative.

Walter Nathan

*The artist serves humanity
by feeding its hungry spirit
in as real a sense as if he fed
its hungry bodies.*

Sylvia Shaw Judson

When countered with the excuse that more seminaries are not addressing this area of concern because of their "chronic state of poverty,"[16] Nathan puts forth a challenge to the great foundations or leading art collectors to endow a chair or establish a "Center of Christian Art." Such a place could provide ministers and Christian educators with an introduction to the rich heritage we have as well as address some of the problems.

In the twenty five years since Nathan's book, there has been, both at the national and local level, an increasing attention to the arts on the part of the church and religious institutions. The following examples reflect this interest:

• The **Society for the Arts, Religion and Contemporary Culture** (ARC) now celebrating its twenty-fifth year, was one of the early efforts to draw clergy and artists together. Amos Wilder and Paul Tillich were among the original founders. The Society meets three times a year.

• In 1977 the **United Church of Christ** passed a resolution entitled "Affirmation of the Arts." This denomination has established a "Fellowship in the Arts" which seeks to encourage and empower local congregations to take art seriously in the ministry and life of the people of faith (see Appendix 1).

• Begun in 1977, the **Institute in Culture and Creation Spirituality** is directed by Matthew Fox, a Dominican priest. The Institute, located in Oakland, California, offers a nine month program of study which seeks to integrate art, cosmology, spirituality, and theology in the Western mystical Christian heritage. The Institute graduates fifty master's students each year from this program. In addition, the Institute presents summer workshops (on the east and west coast), offering participants an opportunity to explore their own creativity in a spiritually liberating and supportive context.

• **Wesley Theological Seminary** in Washington, D.C. has had Artists-in-Residence since 1980 and, in 1984, founded a Center for the Arts and Religion. Courses offered in the Seminary curriculum range from the theoretical, "Visual Arts and Proclamation: From the Catacombs to Citicorp," to the practical, "Contemplative Drawing, A Path to the Fuller Self." A studio visual arts practicum offers the student creative expression through paint, fabric (vestments, banners, paraments), clay, wood, etc., with theological focus. A course in the arts is now a degree requirement.

• **The Graduate Theological Union** in Berkeley, California, has established a Doctoral program in Theology and the Arts and has a full-time professor of "Christianity and the Arts." Fifty-five courses relating Christianity and the arts are offered during the four-year seminary curriculum. Each summer three weeklong workshops on the arts in worship and spirituality are presented.

• **Yale Divinity School**, through its Institute of Sacred Music and the program of Religion and the Arts, offers degree programs to train church leaders in music, liturgy, literature, and the arts.

• **Princeton Theological Seminary,** as part of its Continuing Education Program, has offered a Seminar on Theology and the Arts for several years, led by Dr. Theodore Gill. John and Jane Dillenberger were co-leaders of the course in the fall of 1985.

• In the summer of 1985 a week long workshop on "Spirituality and the Arts" was sponsored by the **Presbyterian School of Christian Education** in Richmond, Virginia, with Dr. John Westerhoff as the key speaker.

• There is an **Interfaith Forum on Religion, Art and Architecture** based in Washington, D.C. It is a national, interfaith organization of architects, church building committees, artists and craft persons, clergy, and other interested members who work to im-

I want to paint men and women with that something of the eternal which the halo used to symbolize.

Vincent Van Gogh

Art, for the artists of earlier times, was one of the wings of love; religion was the other. Art and religion provide humanity with all the certainties that it needs.

Auguste Rodin

*[Rothko's paintings] produce a to-
tal environment in which the ob-
server is enveloped, an impression
different but comparable to that
produced by the orchestration of
space in great Baroque churches
or in Gothic churches by the magical suffusion of color from sunlit,
stained glass windows. The chapel
in Houston, with its great panels
of glowing and shifting dusky red,
invites the participant to silent
and concentrated meditation.*

David Piper

*And so at different points along
the road are the different arts,
saying what they are best able to
say and in the language which is
peculiarly their own. Despite, or
perhaps thanks to, the differences between them, there has never
been a time when the arts approached each other more nearly
than they do today, in this later
phase of spiritual development.*

Wassily Kandinsky

prove the aesthetic and functional design of religious space. A national conference is held each year. Excellence in religious art and architecture awards are given at each national confer-ence. Individual annual membership includes receipt of the semi-annual journal *Faith and Forum.*

• A growing number of churches and temples are commission-ing noted contemporary artists for original works of art. The work of sculptor Louise Nevelson graces a chapel at St. Peter's Church in New York City; Robert Motherwell, noted American abstract expressionist, was chosen to do the interior of St. Mark's in the Bowery; the chapel in St. Thomas' Hospital in Houston, Texas, contains fourteen paintings by Mark Rothko and was opened in 1971, one year after his death. Matisse, Leger, Rouault, Chagall, Lipschitz, and Germaine Richier have works in European churches. Many churches commission less well known but professional local or regional artists.

• In 1976 as part of the 41st **International Eucharist Congress** held in Philadelphia, a large exhibit of Liturgical Arts was held. Some of the works in the exhibit were commissioned for this occasion. In the introduction to the exhibit catalog, Victoria Donohue, art critic for the *Philadelphia Inquirer* wrote:

> The effort is being made [in this exhibit] to re-establish the idea that the practice of art can again have organic identity with the life of the world and with worship, which it had for thou-sands of years, before art became a superfluous activity in an industrial age. [17]

• Many local churches hold monthly art shows or sponsor arts festivals. As an example, following the 1983 Festival of the Arts in Worship sponsored by the **Dumbarton United Methodist Church** in Washington, D.C., the committee printed a Directory of Liturgical Artists who were available for commissions from churches. The wide range of arts is impressive. Included were fiber arts, calligraphy, mosaics, graphics, needle-point, glass and wood design, pottery, sculpture, painting, murals, and stained glass. Leadership for workshops in dance, clowning, mime, drama, puppets, and hymn writing was also offered.

• **First Church of Christ** (Congregational) in Springfield, Massachusetts, has opened a permanent art gallery which features major exhibitions of area artists and is open to the public through the week. It is funded by the Springfield Council for the Arts, First Church, voluntary donations, and commissions on sale of art.

• The **University Christian Church** in Austin, Texas, through an Endowment for Creative Ministry, is offering a three year series on the theme "Eighth Day of Creation." Painting and sculpture were highlighted in the fall of 1986, with thirteen invited artists drawn from across the United States and representing Catholic, Jewish, and Protestant faiths. The 1987 theme concentrated on theater and film, while the 1988 theme will be music and dance.

• The College of Notre Dame in Belmont, California, has established the **Archives of Modern Christian Art** to serve artists, scholars, clergy, and others. The Archives emphasizes research over other activities such as teaching or production, however the work of collecting and cataloging does not preclude projects which could support Archive activities.

• In December, 1985, a consultation on **The Arts and Theological Education** was held at Emory University. Artists, scholars, and administrators were invited to consider ways of integrating the arts more fully into the seminaries' curricula. One presentation, by Wilson Yates, was entitled "The State of the Arts in Theological Education," and reported much more already going on than was originally supposed. Another paper, delivered

The Emory Arts Consultation may well be a harbinger of a new marriage between theology and the arts...Most likely it will not be like the medieval church's calm but fruitful marriage between art and theology. I suspect, instead, that it will either prove to be a marriage of convenience (seminary boards and administrators, noting the interest, will add one new department and place one more requirement on the already harassed student), or there will be an attempt at a genuine integration, a genuine becoming of one flesh. If the latter were to happen, theological education and art would be in for a stormy marriage indeed.

Ronald Goetz

by John Dillenberger, was entitled "The Visual Arts and Christian Thought: Historic Contemporary Issues and a Plea for Wider Horizons." That such a consultation was held at all fosters high hope that there will be new energy to press for a recovery of the arts for the life of the church.

• The **Schuyler Institute for Worship and the Arts,** located in San Carlos, California, has since 1984 provided interdenominational resources for the integration of creative arts and effective worship. Led by a Board of Directors comprised of working artists in many disciplines, the Institute seeks to promote interaction between Christian artists, arts organizations, clergy, seminaries, and congregations. In July 1987, the Institute co-sponsored with the Boston University School of Theology a workshop entitled *The Languages of Worship*, a workshop later presented at Princeton University. Such conferences, consultation (call-in and on-site), and a periodical, *Let the People Worship*, provide a structure through which this organization seeks to minister to the needs of local churches in the area of worship and the arts.

The above sampling, while by no means exhaustive, indicates the breadth and depth of human energy seeking an active means to reawaken the siblings art and religion to their mutual heritage. As this energy percolates through both Christianity and society-at-large, it will eventually touch nearly all humanity. At present, however, the energy operates in mostly isolated pockets of activity. These pockets of activity are nearly always found surrounding an individual artist, or, less often, a pastor through whom the mutual heritage of religion and art can be transmitted. The church-at-large has begun to take note of this activity, and some encouraging signs are appearing. The newly merged Evangelical Lutheran Church in America has now placed a faculty member in Worship in each of this denomination's seminaries. The newly merged Presbyterian Church

(USA) will have a denominational staff position in Worship and the Arts in place during 1988. Hopefully this change is evidence of better things to come.

CHAPTER 4

ART AND THE CHURCH'S LIFE AND MISSION

Having noted some signs of openness by the church to the arts, let us consider certain areas of the church's life and mission for which the arts give us new insights and challenge. Rightly understood, the arts and the creative process have implications for the church's worship, educational programs, priestly, and prophetic roles.

WORSHIP

Worship is central to Christian life. It lies at the very heart of the church's mission. To be concerned about worship is to be concerned about how we approach the deepest reality that we know, how we enter into and respond to this awareness. What happens here affects all else that we do.

What do we see when we look in on a typical Protestant service of worship? We have the word spoken, the word read, and the word sung. We come to "hear the sermon" and "listen to the music." What are we to do with Marshall McLuhan's assertion that modern man is "post literate"[18] or with Father Aiden Nichols' suggestion that we are passing out of a primacy of the word into a primacy of the image?[19]

Television, with all its pros and cons, has caused a dramatic change in the way we perceive reality. No longer is reality mediated through cold print, in a sequential and linear pattern, but instantaneously and involving several senses at once. When watching a television event we are plunged into an experience which taps into our senses of feeling, hearing, and seeing.

Note the following example from a letter a man wrote to the public television station in Philadelphia:

The time is close at hand when mankind will see that...it now stands biologically between the alternative of suicide and worship.

Teilhard de Chardin

By and large, Protestant worship is still in the realm of the communication revolution of the 16th century...After four hundred and fifty years the times have changed, most of all within the last twenty years. We must realize that people...are accustomed to much more immediate forms of communication than words read from a book. And consequently the forms by which worship is expressed must change too.

James White

Thanks for Solomon Northrup's "Odyssey." The program's power froze me to my seat for nearly two hours. I didn't melt until the final ten minutes when my eyes flowed with tears. [20]

A service of worship will seem subdued and restrained, lacking in vitality if only words are used. Particularly is this true for the younger generation. When a past-thirty adult misses church he will ask, "What did he say?" – meaning "What was the sermon about?" The under-thirty adult is more likely to ask, "What happened?" [21]

One area of change must be in worship environments. Our churches in recent generations have stressed comfort and security – cushioned pews and air conditioning. Amidst it all there seems to be an unstated dictum: "No burning bushes, mind you, just soft and pleasant indirect lighting!" [22] We need to bring the vibrancy of color, texture, sound, and movement into praise and worship. The arts can help us take worship out of the routine and expected into a place of wonder and celebration.

As we plan for services of worship, we can be mindful of the *languages* of worship. The Schuyler Institute for Worship and the Arts, in its workshops on worship, lead participants to experience the languages of worship, among them:

verbal	Words spoken, sung, and prayed
sonic	Sounds and silences, including music
visual	Use of color and form in physical space
kinesthetic	Movement, gesture, posture, and motion

Knowing the possibilities of the languages will enable us to help people truly experience worship, not just attend a worship service.

John Westerhoff comments that "the function of artistic expression is to illumine and draw us deeper into life's depths. The arts incarnate our experience of mystery, wonder and awe and thereby aid us to encounter the holy and sacred." [23] One has to ask, do we really want to encounter the holy and sacred? Would we rather not be "snugly wrapped away from the chills of the tremendum"? [24] Annie Dillard, writing in *Teaching a Stone to Talk,* reminds us how Israel heard God speak and found it too loud (Exodus 20:18-21), and "it scared them witless." They asked Moses to beg God not to speak that way. Moses took the message to God and now "it is difficult to undo our own damage, and to recall to our presence that which we have asked to leave…We doused the burning bush and cannot rekindle it; we are lighting matches in vain under every green tree." [25] Art forms can serve as "symbol-painted curtains" which both give meaning to the 'tremendum' and protect us from its terror.

In his autobiographical novel *The Seven Storey Mountain*, Thomas Merton tells us how he discovered Christ. It happened one summer while he was travelling around Europe on his own.

> I don't know how it began –
> I found myself looking
> into churches…
>
> The effect of the discovery
> was tremendous.
> What a thing it was to come upon…
> an art that was…
> urgent in all that it had to say…
> I began to haunt the churches.

And now for the first time in my life
I began to find out something
of who this Person was
that men called Christ.
The saints of those forgotten days
had left upon the walls of their church
a word
which…I was able
in some measure to apprehend…

But above all,
the most real and most immediate source
(of my new knowledge)…
was Christ himself,
present in those churches…
And it was he
who was teaching me
who he was,
more directly
than I was capable of realizing…

And I brought
the New Testament…
and I read more and more
of the Gospels,
and my love for the old churches…
and their mosaics
grew from day to day.
Soon I was no longer visiting them
for art…
something else attracted me.
A kind of interior peace. [26]

How much art in our places of worship today is "urgent in all that
it has to say?" How much brings Christ's presence into immedi-

*…Art is not an end in itself. It
introduces the soul into a higher
spiritual order, which it expresses
and in some sense explains. Music
and art and poetry attune the soul
to God because they induce a kind
of contact with the Creator and
Ruler of the Universe.*

Thomas Merton

ate experience? How much leads one beyond the art form to that "interior peace?" How many churches are without any artistic nourishment of the senses and the spirit?

Unfortunately, even the art that has been present in churches has often been of questionable quality. Who can know the damage done by the poor religious art often found in our places of worship? "A cold, neglected church can evoke a sense of fear, indifference, even hostility. A religious picture on a wall calendar may shape a child's mental image of Christ long before he has learned anything about the Christian faith." [27]

Too much of what we find deserves the term "kitsch" – that which degrades religious truth by its sentimentality and trivialization.

It was the desire to bring the best contemporary artists into the service of the church that led Father M. A. Couturier to build the church at Assy, France. Artists invited to submit works included Rouault, Leger, Lipchitz, Chagall, Matisse, Braque, Bonnard, Lucrat, and Germaine Richier. Controversial as it was (two of the artists were Jewish, one an atheist, and another Marxist), one cannot argue with the passionate motive of Father Couturier's efforts. In his words,

> We were tired of always seeing in our churches the most mediocre examples of painting and sculpture. In the long run we thought this mediocrity could only result in seriously altering the religious psychology of clergy and worshippers alike. We were also aware that unbelievers, comparing these works to the great Christian art of the past, would inevitably question the vitality of a Faith and a Church that could remain content with them.

The building of the church at Assy and a few other instances of churches using the work of modern artists led Aniela Jaffe, writ-

---

Protestantism, with its accent on auditory rather than liturgical or sacramental space, is conscious of forms, but uninterested, uneducated, or suspicious of the sensuous nature of the visual arts of painting and sculpture. Protestantism has lived so long without the visual that the loss of that human and spiritual resource is not even recognized as an issue.

John Dillenberger

When one looks into the window of a store which sells devotional art objects, one can't help wishing the iconoclasts had won.

W. H. Auden

ing in *Man and His Symbols,* to say,

> The utterly unexpected has happened: the Church has
> become the patron of modern art. We need mention
> here All Saints at Basle, with windows by Alfred Manessi-
> er; Assy Church with pictures by a large number of mod-
> ern artists; the Matisse chapel at Vence; and the Church
> at Audincourt, which has works by Jean Bazaine and the
> French artist Fernand Leger.

> The admission of modern art to the Church means more
> than an act of broadmindedness on the part of its patron.
> It is symbolic of the fact that the part played by modern
> art in relation to Christianity is changing.

Nevertheless, there is still a scarcity of contemporary works of a
religious nature. Does this suggest that the church's message
is no longer capable of inspiring creative minds? More likely,
says Nathan, it is that artists have been disappointed, if not at
times humiliated, in their experiences with the church. They
have felt ignored and rebuffed and most have concluded that it
is best to avoid Christian themes if they wish to earn a liveli-
hood.

Richard Caemmerer challenges us to find the growing number
of artists with special visions and gifts who can help the church
communicate its reason for being in the most dynamic way possible. "If ever the church needed the best tools for celebration,
the most creative energies with which to carry out its mission, it
needs them now." [28]

Almost twenty five years ago Walter Nathan wrote that there
were "stirrings of a vital new Christian art in our own country and
particularly in Europe. Great exhibitions have given proof of
the astonishing scope and richness of work in every medium
being done in many places by dedicated artists." [29] Is any con-

*Artists have been accusing
churches of nonsupport while
churches accuse artists of lack of
interest. There seems enough
guilt for everyone, but the guilt is
not producing either excellent
spaces for worship or artistic
expresssions of faith. It is enough,
sadly, to realize that an immense
majority of buildings and spaces
devoted to praise, meditation,
discussion and celebration of our
life in Christ continues to reflect a
life uninspired, unlovely, uncaring
and uninteresting.*

Richard Caemmerer

sistent effort being made to find these artists? Such a search should be given high priority.

The spirit of artists who work in our churches is given voice by Nancy Chinn, a painter whose art focuses on sanctuary space and faith expression:

> I want my church to encourage me as an artist, to trust my vision-making process. I want to find true joy and meaning in sharing that gift with others. I want to face the challenges of integrating my faith with the materials of my culture. I want to search for that vision in collective dialogue so that I too can be enlightened and refreshed by that process. [30]

Sometimes, artists are literally going in search of the church. Ben Long, a North Carolina artist, studied fresco painting in Florence, Italy. Upon his return he wanted to paint in churches. He traversed the state, concentrating primarily on larger towns and cities, to convince a church to let him paint a religious fresco on the wall. He met with no response. Finally, as a last resort before returning to Italy, he approached the pastor of two very small Episcopal churches in the mountains of North Carolina with his offer of painting the murals for only the cost of the materials.

An agreement was reached and in the summer of 1978 some twenty artists from all over America and several foreign countries arrived to help Long paint the frescoes: "The Last Supper" and "Mary Great with Child." The entire area responded with food and housing for the artists. Models for the disciples were drawn from the surrounding community. These remarkable frescoes are visited by thousands of people yearly. Not only did this work help in the "rebirth of a mountain parish," [31] but affected the economy of the whole area and left a legacy of art for generations to come. Long was presented with the pre-

I want to give our church songs yet unsung, environments yet unimagined, words not yet forged to poems, dances not yet choreographed, and all the other dazzling testimonies to the creative power of the Spirit at work among God's people. I want to bring the warmth and disclosure of art to worship, to bring unwordable joy to the sacraments, to personalize the pain and sorrow of the reality of crucifixion, and to proclaim a promise of resurrection that touches the whole center of our lives, not merely our intellects.

Nancy Chinn

stigious Leonardo da Vinci International Art Award for his work in these two small churches and in Europe.

Bo Bartlett, a young Philadelphia painter, was greatly influenced by Ben Long, whom he met in Florence. A highly respected portrait and landscape painter, Bartlett began to approach a number of churches in the Philadelphia area, offering to paint a large mural in their church only in exchange for the cost of the materials. In 1984 he painted, for St. Luke's Episcopal Church in Kensington, "Festival of Shelter." [32] The mural was completed in three months of working in the church with the canvas stretched and mounted on the wall. St. John's Episcopal Church of Bala Cynwyd also has a mural in the sanctuary painted by Bartlett entitled "The Transfiguration."

Finding the artists is one thing; at the same time churches need guidance on *how* to commission original art so that the relationship between artist and church can be as fruitful and satisfying as possible (See Appendix 2.) Surely, faith and artistic talent can indeed share a natural alliance with one another, as in former times!

EDUCATION

WAYS OF LEARNING AND TEACHING

Neuroscientists have provided a conceptual base for understanding the right and left brain theories of learning and understanding reality. The majority of our educational materials and methods have relied on left brain modality, i.e. verbal and analytical thinking, objective and conceptual learning. Our teaching and learning, both in the church and other educational institutions, has been largely an intellectual activity communicated primarily through the printed and spoken word.

To have mastered something with the intellect gives us the illusion that one is in possession of the thing itself.

Carl Jung

The lack of the arts of the eye in the context of Protestant life is, though historically understandable, systematically untenable and practically regrettable.

Paul Tillich

Almost without knowing it, our exaggerated esteem for language has led us to a place where we assume that "verbal statements provide the primary or the exclusive route to truth."[33] The neglect or even intentional disregard of right-brain activity, i.e. non-verbal, holistic, intuitive, feeling, has resulted in an alienation from the deepest centers of life.

"Half a brain is better than none: A whole brain would be better," says Betty Edwards in her book *Drawing on the Right Side of the Brain*.[34] If we have two ways of knowing and two ways of processing information, we short-change ourselves by cultivating only half of what God has given us. Cultivating the right brain will bring us more in touch with our capacities for visualizing and imaging, for creativity, intuition, and inventiveness.

Many educators and theologians have expressed the need for the non-verbal, affective approaches to education. Maria Harris, professor at Andover Newton Theological Seminary, teaches a course entitled "The Aesthetic and Religious Education." She views her course as an essential one in the seminary curriculum. It serves, she feels, an "integrating, holistic and digesting" purpose as it "provides an oasis where people can, in stillness, let their understanding, their intellect, and their feelings come together without pressure...The aesthetic is a reminder that more than the rational exists and that it nurtures and feeds the human spirit if we let it."[35]

The value of such courses being included in the Seminary curriculum is evidenced by a recent curriculum piece for youth entitled, *Gift of God – Gift to God: Living the Word Through Artistry*.[36] It was written by Wendy Ward who acknowledged with special thanks the contribution made by her professor, Dr. Harris, in a course on aesthetics while she was at Andover Newton Seminary.

Sara Little, Professor of Christian Education at Union Theologi-

The notion that education is about educating the left brain alone is obsolete and inherently violent. It does violence to the individual and ultimately to society itself.

Matthew Fox

The inborn capacity to understand through the eyes has been put to sleep and must be awakened.

Rudolf Arnheim

cal Seminary in Richmond, Virginia, in her book, *To Set One's Heart – Belief and Teaching in the Church*, calls for a teaching style which she describes as "encounter" or indirect communication. She acknowledges that it is hard to find models for teaching in this way, but feels this approach has unique potential for the work of the church.

What can be done to encourage greater use of this "encounter" style of teaching? Little suggests:

> Because it depends so largely on the intuition of the teacher, about the only thing one can do is encourage the teacher to enrich her/his own life with all types of art, to 'sense' where students are, and at appropriate moments to build in exposure to art, with the use of silence as well as free response.[37]

Such a suggestion presupposes that the ministers and Christian educators who train teachers will themselves know of the rich resources available.

STEWARDS OF A RICH HERITAGE OF CHRISTIAN ART

Certainly within the educational settings of our churches, we need to be passing along the amazing richness of our heritage in religious art. In the introduction to the book, *The Bible and Its Painters*, Lawrence Gowing comments about the astonishing abundance of painting that illustrates the Bible:

> There is nothing like this flood of narrative painting, nothing so imaged yet specific, pictured exactly and in detail, then reimaged, over and over down the centuries. There is nothing resembling it among all the culture of man.[38]

Such painting through the years met a devotional need and at

Too often we have sought convergent rather than divergent thinking, have rewarded analytical rather than metaphorical thinking, have worked with outlines rather than with images...

Work is needed on the development of creative imagination, giving persons time to brood, to let the unconscious work in a kind of 'wrestling of the spirit' in a relating of fleeting images and ideas in some form that can be offered to others.

Sara Little

times served as instruction for the illiterate, but mostly, suggests Gowing, it met the need for "imaginative nourishment." Every age has need of that!

Rembrandt alone depicted more than 850 Biblical stories and themes in various media. Yet how many churches know of and avail themselves of reproductions (prints and slides) of Rembrandt's paintings and etchings or work of other artists which can be secured from the National Gallery of Art in Washington, D.C., for as little as fifty cents each.

Slides of religious works by the following artists can be purchased from the American Library Color Slide Company in New York City at modest cost: [39]

Blake	Caravaggio	Durer
El Greco	Michelangelo	Nolde
Raphael	Rembrandt	Rothko
Rouault	Rubens	Titian

From the same address one can order slides of early Christian Art (the catacombs, the Ravenna Mosaics of the 5th and 6th century, etc.), "Russian Icon Painting," "Christian Symbolism," and "Great Images of Christ in the History of Art" – all of which will provide sources of the artistic language of the Christian faith. Imagine the enrichment such a resource library of visual images could be to church school teachers and ministers!

A resource of visual images can be utilized in many ways. A study of church history from the early church through the medieval period and into the twentieth century, could be greatly enriched by a study of Christian art and architecture. Our historical understandings have relied primarily on verbal texts, and need to be complemented by visual texts. The work of John Cook [40] and Margaret Miles [41] can help to chart the way.

The universality of the Christian message is most eloquently proclaimed by Christian artists of all races and cultures. Contemporary Japanese artist Sadao Watanabe has created a remarkable witness of the vitality of his Christian faith through his countless renderings of the stories of the Bible. Feeling acutely the artistic poverty of his fellow Christians in Japan, Watanabe has devoted his life to fill this void, convinced that "Theology will not take deep root in the Japanese soil if it is merely an import." Warm response to his sensitive portrayals reach far beyond his native Japan.

The relevancy of the Gospel message to contemporary issues can be experienced anew as we see it through the artists' eyes of the peasants of Solentiname, Nicaragua. In the book, *The Gospel in Art by the Peasants of Solentiname,* "both Christ and Mary are peasants...seen in the familiar settings of Solentiname, with its thatched-roofed buildings, bright blue waters, and lush vegetation starred by brilliant flowers...(their paintings) show forth their deep conviction that Jesus lives and is indeed present among them...that the Gospel is the living word of the living God heard in their world." [42] Our own lukewarmness and complacency can be shaken by this rendering of the Gospel by humble peasants.

The portrayal of Biblical women in the art of times past can help us rediscover obscured traditions of the place of women in the church. Elisabeth Moltmann-Wendel in her book *The Women Around Jesus* collects for us paintings of Martha defeating the dragon, Mary Magdalene preaching, and Mary and Martha painted into the Garden of Gethsemane scene (awake!) by Fra Angelico. This visual history suggests that women enjoyed a greater respect and authority than we have supposed. [43]

The art image can be used for meditation. A slide of a Russian icon, Carravagio's "Supper at Emmaus," Rembrandt's "Head of Christ," or Leonardo's "Last Supper" can be projected for a period of silent meditation, inviting people to really stay with a work of art for a sustained period.

Art can enrich Bible study. Hans-Ruedi Weber, Director of Biblical studies at the World Council of Churches, in his book *Experiments in Bible Study*, suggests the value of "*seeing* God's image" as well as "*hearing* God's message." He encourages leaders of Bible studies to use visual elements in their presentations, especially for meditation on a Biblical passage or for fixing insights of Bible study in the mind and heart. Artists' work, he writes, "can open our minds and hearts and eyes to discover dimensions in God's message which a purely literary study of texts will never disclose." [44] Two of his books, *On a Friday Noon,* and *Immanuel: the Coming of Jesus in Art and the Bible*, provide artists' visual interpretations of the Biblical message from many centuries and different cultures.

We need to strengthen our discipline of seeing and what better place to start than in our church schools! It will provide a less travelled way to enter into Christian truth, and will give a balance to our verbally oriented educational programs.

ART IN A PRIESTLY ROLE

Art, beyond having a valuable place in our educational programs, can move into another area, more difficult to describe. Some have called it the "sacramental power" of art, or speak of its healing or transforming power, even of its "revelatory power."

Well known are deep religious experiences which are prompted by the "word." Saint Augustine's "take and read" or Martin Luther's understanding of the words – "The just shall live by faith" – are two examples of verbal revelations. Margaret Miles in her book *Image as Insight*, reminds us of numerous accounts of persons converted by seeing rather than hearing. Powerful visual experiences with a crucifix, painting, or vision, dramatically changed and altered the lives of St. Francis, Saint Catherine of Sienna, Lady Julian of Norwich, and others. [45] To this one could add the contemporary experience of Teilhard de Chardin which he describes in "The Picture." His account is of an "intense vision which gave light and peace to his life." [46]

One remembers the story in the Old Testament of the bronze serpent made by Moses at the command of God. When looked upon by the people of Israel, the image had power to heal the wounds caused by the fiery serpents. Seeing an image, made with human hands, somehow resulted in healing. And this becomes the symbol of the medical profession, and was, of course, a prefiguration of the Cross.

And as Moses lifted up the serpent in the wilderness, so must the Son of man be lifted up, that whoever believes in him (looks on him) may have eternal life.

John 3:14

Sometimes there have been "life-affecting encounters with art" which did not derive from a specifically "religious image." Quaker Dorothea Blom describes an experience in the Metropolitan Museum in New York in her Pendle Hill Pamphlet, *Encounters with Art:*

> For many months I had been in a state of acute inner crisis. On this day I found myself submerged in a cloud of density. I wandered aimlessly, finding vague comfort in anonymity among familiar surroundings, just psychologically and physically drifting. Looking back, I cannot recall the minute of change. There I stood, before a painting I had never noticed before, with floodgates of compassion wide open and all the world drenched in healing light. The whole world and I were forgiven and connected up in a lovingness not our own. Not forgiven for special offenses – simply forgiven.
>
> For weeks I lived in an aftermath of that flood. All my visu-

al experience inspired feelings of wonder and awe. Then, after a few weeks, this seeing began to fade. The world started to look more familiar, more routine. Yet I had been released from inner impasse and re-entered my life from a new inner position...

How could I drop the matter there? I felt that everything I ever knew had become unimportant and I could start learning all over again. Teeming questions wooed me...What happened that day in the museum? Why? Who else had stumbled into life-affecting encounters with art? Could one build a relationship to art to serve healing processes and transformations? How?[47]

Novelist Iris Murdoch, in her story, *The Bell*, tells of a visit by Dora to the National Gallery in London. The artworks before her bestow a sense of reality beyond herself, and the experience is spoken of in terms of revelation. The paintings "spoke to her kindly, yet in sovereign tones," and Dora felt that she had had a revelation. "She looked at the radiant, sombre, powerful canvas of Gainsborough and felt a sudden desire to go down on her knees before it, embracing it, shedding tears...She gave a last look at the paintings, still smiling as one might smile in a temple, favoured, encouraged, loved."[48]

Neither of these experiences was related to a religious painting – yet some quality of the work served as an entry way, a meeting place between the individual and God. It is the same quality of an icon which points beyond itself, through which one glimpses, touches, a transcendent reality.

One moves cautiously in this area of the power of art, yet to refuse to be open to these possibilities would not be true to the church's historic traditions and contemporary experience.

ART AS CREATIVE EXPRESSION

Fostering creativity is another important area in which the church needs to be involved and in which the arts may play a primary role. This is the other side of indirect communication, says Sara Little, "when a person expresses the self in art rather than responds to a work of art."[49] Creativity is an essential human activity, part of our being created in the image of God. Hildegard of Bingen gave expression to this thought in the 11th century:

> God be praised in his handiwork:
>   Humankind.
>   And so,
>   humankind
> full of all creative possibilities,
>   is God's work.
>
> Humankind alone,
>   is called to assist God.
> Humankind is called to co-create.[50]

Matthew Fox writes of this important theme of creativity in the theology of Meister Eckhart, mystic of the 13th century:

> God is being driven to generate or give birth...The essence of God is to give birth...We too are artists as God is. We are heirs of God, heirs of the fearful creative power of God...God is, as it were compelled to be an artist...Our divinization requires our creativity. One cannot be divine without being creative and fruitful.[51]

In the very act of creating something, and it need not be "great art," a truth may come to one which would not be discovered any other way. "Often the hands know how to solve a riddle

Creative experience is just as religious as is prayer or asceticism...its roots go into the deepest depths.

[There is an] eschatalogical element in creative power that stems from discontent with the world as it is. It anticipates the transfiguration of the world. This is the meaning of art, of art of any kind. Human creative power is not human only, it is divine-human. All the great creative works of men enter into the Kingdom of God.

Nicholas Berdyaev

Art after all is but an extension of language to the expression of sensations too subtle for words.

Robert Henri

Painting is not done to decorate apartments...It is an instrument of war for attack and defence against the enemy.

Picasso

The churches believed they had all the answers. But in believing that they had all the answers they deprived the answers of their meaning. These answers were no longer understood because the questions were no longer understood, and this was the churches' fault. They did not do what the existentialist artist did. They did not ask the question over again as they should have out of the experience of despair in industrial society. The churches did not ask the question, and therefore their answers, all the religious answers Christianity has in its creeds, became empty because the questions were not vivid any more as they were in the periods in which these answers were given.

Paul Tillich

with which the intellect has wrestled in vain," wrote Carl Jung. [52] Persons who have worked with clay or paint under certain conditions can testify to the truth of that statement. And if one can be at ease with some form of creative expression – be it movement, song, clay, paint, poetry – what a resource it becomes for prayer and meditation, or just putting some joy and order into the confusion of life!

Enabling both young and old to tap into their creative birthright is no small thing. To recover faith in one's own creativity, the artist within all of us, can rekindle the sparks of hope and vision that our tired civilization needs.

PROPHETIC MINISTRY

To be interested in art is not to turn our backs on the needs of the world or neglect the prophetic voice of the church.

Matthew Fox links creating art with social justice. This is not elitist art, art for investment, consumption, or entertainment. This is art that recreates the social order. To be able to create, suggests Fox, means one refuses to be a victim. It is the process of working with materials of art that brings this truth about. One engages in a "passion to make and make again in a society that has enthroned unmaking or the making by others instead of making ourselves." [53]

Fox tells the story of a Catholic Sister in Chicago who worked with women in prison. She told the women she had funds which could either get them a good lawyer to review their cases and possibly get them out sooner; or she could bring in a welder to teach them welding so they could have a skill when they left; or she could get a dancer and painter to come teach them to dance and paint. Ninety-five percent wanted a dancer or painter! Why? Because, they said, it would be the first time in their lives they would have a chance to express themselves. [54] The poor need more than freedom from hunger. They need freedom to create, to construct, to wonder, and to venture. This is where art links up with social justice.

A prophetic task of the church is always to speak a relevant word to the needs of the society in which it serves. Understanding the mindset of a generation is essential to presenting the "good news" of the Gospel. Paul Tillich felt that modern art performed a religious function because it helped the church rediscover the basic questions which he believed the church had lost.

Once having understood the questions, Christian symbols could become understandable again. Tillich acknowledges the value which modern art had for him: "I must confess that I have not learned from any theological book as much as I learned from these pictures of the great modern artists who broke through into the realm out of which symbols are born. And you cannot understand theology without understanding symbols." [55]

SYMBOLS

The critical importance of symbols is one to which the church must give serious attention, for it relates art to the prophetic tradition. Carl Jung, writing in *Man and His Symbols* stated that:

> (Man) has freed himself from 'superstition' (or so he believes) but in the process he has lost his spiritual values to a *positively dangerous degree*. His moral and spiritual tradition has disintegrated and he is now paying the price for this break up in world-wide disorientation and disassociation...But we have never really understood what we have lost, for *our spiritual leaders unfortunately were*

The art of free society consists first in the maintenance of a symbolic code; and secondly in the fearlessness of revision, to secure that the code serves those purposes which satisfy as enlightened reason. Those societies which cannot combine reverence to their symbols with freedom of revision, must ultimately decay either from anarchy, or from the slow atrophy of life stifled by useless shadows.

Alfred North Whitehead

more interested in protecting their institution than in understanding the mystery that symbols present. [56]

Why are symbols so important and what do they do? Tillich wrote in *Theology of Culture* that symbols open up "levels of reality which otherwise are hidden and cannot be grasped in any other way. Every symbol opens up a level of reality for which non-symbolic speaking is inadequate." [57] "Symbols," stated Jung, "are natural attempts to reconcile and reunite opposites within the psyche." [58]

"A symbol 'presences' as opposed to re-presents" says Diane Apostolos-Cappadona. [59] A symbol is not the same as that which it symbolizes but participates in its meaning and power.

"How do symbols arise and how do they come to an end?" "Out of what womb are symbols born?" These questions, raised by Tillich, are of central importance. Symbols can lose their force; become shallow, dry up. A symbol dies when it no longer says anything. [60]

What is our present situation? To T. S. Eliot, it is:

> A heap of broken images, where the sun beats,
> And the dead tree gives no shelter, the cricket
> no relief;
> And the dry stone no sound of water. [61]

The twentieth century is littered with broken symbols, said Tillich. Jung maintained that our age suffers from starvation of symbols and that the symbols we have no longer have a numinous quality.

Though some writers question the validity of the Christian faith for any modern mind, Jung continued to explore the deeper meanings of that faith. Jung wrote about Christ as a symbol of the Self. A lengthy treatise on "Transformation Symbolism in the Mass" and a full book on *Symbols of Transformation* were part of his important writings. He was fond of quoting Tertullian's statement, "The soul is naturally Christian." He credited Meister Eckhart with helping him find the key to the unconscious:

> The art of letting things happen, action in nonaction, letting go of oneself, as taught by Meister Eckhart, became for me the key opening the door to the way. [62]

Symbols are not intentionally invented nor are they constructed by the intellect. They come when we are sensitive to the symbolic dimension, when we have the courage to be open to new depths. It is the "artists, the poets and playwrights, and above all the creative scientists who reach out toward a larger contact with the mystery of reality" asserts Ira Progoff. [63] Gerald Slusser writes similarly, "The artist is unusually sensitive to the symbols of the psyche and not infrequently 'leads' the culture into new mythic symbols, the foundation of new paradigms." [64]

Writing from the perspective of Biblical interpretation, Walter Brueggemann, in his book *The Prophetic Imagination*, states that it is the task of the prophet to offer symbols that are adequate to the time in which he lives. The prophet reactivates out of the historical past symbols which have had meaning. The Exodus is such a symbol for it declares to "all would-be Pharaohs that the Exodus is a catastrophic ending of what seemed forever." [65]

Further, says Brueggemann, the prophet must bring to public expression the very fears and terrors that have been denied so long and suppressed so deeply that the people are not even aware that they are there. There is a pervasive numbness which keeps Israel from knowing the depths of her despair and

It is just possible that with their extra-sensitized intuition, artists may have unconsciously predicted the discovery of atomic energy long before the 'bomb' became a familiar household word, for the history of break-up in art antedates the history of nuclear break-up.

Katherine Kuh

The arts are dangerous because they might make people feel for their fellows...Knowledge has entered the head and immediately been covered over by that psychic numbing, by paralysis and despair. Intellectual knowledge is swiftly followed by repression of that knowledge.

Denise Levertov

also keeps her immune from her brother's need. The status quo, the "royal consciousness" is invested in numbness. The numbness is manifested in a lack of imagination, a loss of passion and an inability to care or suffer. The prophet Jeremiah can be seen as a "paradigm for those who address the numb and denying posture of people who do not want to know what they have or what their neighbors have." [66] It is not by analytic speech that this numbness is broken. Rather, Jeremiah provides a rich supply of metaphors. By image and poetry he seeks to help Judah know what time it is (Jeremiah chapters 8-10). And it is only when the numbness is broken that something new becomes possible.

When the imagination is choked, so also is our knowledge.

Thomas Aquinas

But the "royal consciousness...is one that shrinks imagination because imagination is a danger. Thus every totalitarian regime is frightened of the artist." [67] It becomes "the vocation of the prophet to keep alive the ministry of imagination." [68] It is the arts, says Denise Levertov, which "can make ideas real, fuse them with feeling, pull them from the realm of abstraction...The function of the imagination is not to take one away from reality, but to make reality real. Intellectual knowledge alone does not do that." [69]

Only as suffering is made audible and visible can any newness break through. Grief must be articulated, pain must be given voice. And who can do that better than the poet, the dancer, the singer, the painter? Maya Angelou, black writer and poet, writes in her autobiography:

> Oh, Black known and unknown poets
> how often have your auctioned pains sustained us?
> If we were a people much given to revealing secrets,
> we might raise monuments,
> and sacrifice to the memories of poets
> but slavery cured us of that weakness.
> It may be enough, however, to have it said that we

survive in exact relation to the dedication of our poets (including preachers, musicians and blues singers).

To be open to new symbols will require courage, trust and community. Of *courage*, Rollo May, in his book *The Courage to Create*, describes creative courage which will discover "new form, new symbols and new patterns on which society can be built...There is profound joy in the realization that we are forming the structure of a new world."[70]

Of *trust*, Matthew Fox writes of "a trust that out of silence, waiting, openness, emptiness one can and will give birth to images."[71]

Of *community*, Andre Malraux insists that "sacred art and religious art can exist only in community, a social group swayed by the same belief (the number nowadays on the increase.)"[72] Delving into the deep places is frightening without a supportive community. And it is the community which must verify new symbols. Wrote Tillich, "even if somebody would try to invent a symbol, as sometimes happens, then it becomes a symbol only if the unconscious of a group says 'yes' to it...that something is opened up by it."[73] Jacques Barzun, toward the end of his book *The Use and Abuse of Art*, predicts, "We may reasonably suppose, therefore, that the new man and his art will not be individual – at least at first – but communal."[74]

Women's search today for new images and symbols relevant to their experience is an excellent illustration of this dynamic. The book *Image Breaking/Image Building* grew out of a workshop for women who gathered from a commitment to make Christian worship more expressive of women's reality. The workshop was generated by both anger and yearning: "*anger* at the language, forms and images that consistently ignore the realities of women's lives and experience; *yearning* to bring the universal dimension of women's experience into the prayer and cele-

While Christian art may contain both priestly and prophetic forms, the latter are nearly absent in church, where they should predominate.

Doug Adams

Seeing through the fabric of texture and flesh into the soul of things, sensing impending change, suffering with humanity, he [the artist] is alone in his creative labors, and like most prophets, he must expect to be stoned and derided, silenced and neglected.

Fritz Eichenberg

In order to maintain the vitality necessary to carry the meaning of faith, religious symbols must be constantly transformed. The process of transformation is epitomized in the work that women are called to do to rid Christianity of the idolatry of the maleness of God. It is accomplished through the active reflection of communities and individuals on questions of faith and its expression in their lives.

Image Breaking/Image Building

...since Christian churches have relinquished the task of providing life-orienting images, secular culture has seized the opportunity of filling the void...they do provide images from which people form self images, values and attitudes...churches, in abdicating responsibility for the training of vision, have failed to provide both life-orienting images and training in their critical appreciation.

Margaret Miles

bration of the worshipping community." [75] For them this required both image breaking and image building and it necessitated community in which this could be done.

Father John Miller, writing in the introduction to the catalog of "Exhibition of Liturgical Arts" held in Philadelphia in 1973, states:

> Maybe many of the symbols which worked in a classical age or a gothic one or a baroque one do not work today; maybe the rapidity of the twentieth century does not give us much chance to step off the merry-go-round to discern whether new symbols are developing. [76]

The foregoing paragraphs suggest that it is critical to make time to explore whether we need only to re-vitalize the old symbols or whether we need new symbols to speak of God in this post-modern world. The late Roger Ortmayer, former editor of *Motive Magazine*, expressed the following conviction some twenty five years ago:

> One of Protestantism's great needs is a powerful symbolization that reveals its faith. The church must seek out the artist who has the talent to create imaginatively in its service. Perhaps this is the most important frontier in church life today. Many believe it is. [77]

Hopefully, many more believe it today.

CHAPTER 5
ARTISTS AND THEIR CALLING

Undoubtedly, artists have much to share. We must not, however, see artists only in terms of their usefulness to the church, as mere "handmaidens for communicating the gospel."[78] "To bring forth art is a calling most simple and severe but at the same time a destiny and thus greater than any of us, more powerful and immeasurable to the end," wrote Rainer Maria Rilke in his book on Rodin.[79] The artist's call comes "with the rigor of an absolute" says Erich Neumann, and "whoever he may be, and wherever he may be, it compels him to travel the road of Abraham, to leave the land of his birth, his mother, and the house of his father, and seek out the land to which the godhead leads him."[80]

Matthew Fox has described the fears with which artists and all creative persons struggle. These fears include fear of death, fear of life, fear of suffering, fear of pleasure, fear of androgyny, and fear of guilt.[81] As artists struggle to integrate the chaos both within themselves and within their society, they are often strained to the utmost. This led Erich Neumann to suggest that the careers of the great artists of our time are all, in greater or lesser degree, calvaries.

The artist is often considered to be an outsider – "condemned to be on the boundary rather than in the comfortable, powerful or acclaimed center of a culture's life," writes Langdon Gilkey.[82] Artists are under pressure to conform, to produce what the market will buy. Artists offer little that a technical, materialistic society considers noteworthy.

Artists are those who wish to leave behind a gift (see Otto Rank, *Art and Artist*.) And the gift is not used up in giving. Thus artists need an audience. They need someone to re-

The need of his times works inside the artist without his wanting it, seeing it, or understanding its true significance. In this sense he is close to the seer, the prophet, the mystic. And it is precisely when he does not represent the existing canon but transforms and overturns it that his function rises to the level of the sacral, for he gives utterance to the authentic and direct revelation of the 'numinosum.'

Erich Neumann

ceive their gifts:

> Even if we have paid a fee at the door of the museum or concert hall, when we are touched by a work of art something comes to us which has nothing to do with the 'price.' True art is a gift which offers to pass through and transform the self. And when we come upon such work we feel gratitude – we are grateful that the artist lived, grateful that he labored in the service of his gifts. [83]

"Did I search for the way so painfully unless to show it to my brothers?" exclaimed Goethe. "Not to be able to give one's gift to those one loves most (is) the only one real deprivation," wrote May Sarton in her *Journal of a Solitude*. "The gift turned inward, unable to be given, becomes a heavy burden, even sometimes a kind of poison. It is as though the flow of life were backed up." [84]

Artists play an important role in bridging divisions between peoples. Because they work from a right-brain orientation, artists search for connections rather than distinctions. Boundaries become blurred and barriers can be overcome. Among the many which could be cited, note the following examples:

• Cultural exchanges agreed upon by the Soviet Union and the United States at the Geneva Summit in the fall of 1985 provided the American people with a rare opportunity to view forty-one post-Impressionist paintings from museums of Leningrad and Moscow. In turn, work from American museums are being sent to Russia.

• "Detente on the Dance Floor" was the title of a newspaper article in the *Philadelphia Inquirer* in June of 1986. It described the meeting of the Pennsylvania Ballet with the Kirov Ballet after a final performance of the latter in Philadelphia. Written in Russian, a banner of welcome stretched across the dance floor

Like so called religious persons, artists can adapt their work so that it merely celebrates current forms of power, so that it merely sanctifies our technical advances, our affluence, our dominance...By this means, however, art will only enlarge the vacuum rather than fill it.

[Artists] are not experts: their importance is not that they know how to do anything useful to anyone but other artists; they don't make instruments for anyone else's use, or even make money or jobs for others. They say, 'Stop, look and see what is real, and be.' In our rushing world, no one has time for this.

Langdon Gilkey

in the International House – "Pennsylvania Ballet – Kirov Ballet: Comrades in Art." Artistic Director of the Pennsylvania Ballet, Robert Weiss, was quoted as saying, "There isn't any difference between us at rock bottom. There are differences between our governments, ideological differences, but artistically, what we do and what they do is exactly the same. We communicate from the heart."

• A newspaper account entitled, "Using Art to Break Down Irish Barriers" described a group of poets and playwrights in England and Ireland. Catholic and Protestant, their energies in exploring together the history and myths of their divided land was causing a surge of creativity and giving hope to greater understanding in that troubled area. [85]

• "Hands Across the Desert," an art exhibit of two hundred pieces of modern Israeli and Egyptian art, was organized by the Congregation Adath Jeshurun in Elkins Park, Pennsylvania, in an effort to foster peace and understanding "at the people level" through an appreciation of each other's art. [86]

Certainly artists have much to offer our society and the religious community. As artists struggle with their sense of isolation, seek to withstand pressures and misunderstandings, and remain faithful to their visions, we can be grateful for their courage, and open to dialogue with their concerns.

There are ideas, insights and experiences which only sound can communicate, others only communicated by movement, others which only color and line can capture. This is why the arts offer insight into God, each other, and ourselves which can be offered in no other way.

Judith Rock

CHAPTER 6

FULL CIRCLE

Is religious art the fruit of another, now outdated, season of the human spirit, or is it and can it be also of this modern age, in which the religious root seems to have lost so much of its magical power or inspiration?...Does there exist today a religious, present-day modern art, the daughter of our time and the twin sister of secular art, which still stimulates and delights the eye, and also the spirit of the man of our century?

Yes,...today we still have artists capable of pitting themselves against the challenges of religious subjects, and we have works of religious art, even if it is not properly sacred, which are rightly spoken about.

We say openly: there still exists...in this arid secularized world of ours...a prodigious capacity of expressing, beyond what is authentically human, the religious, the divine, the Christian.

Paul VI

"Theatre Groups Find Haven in Polish Churches" was the heading of a small news item.[87]   A theatre group called "Theatre of the Eighth Day," after an existence of twenty years, was forced to "liquidate" because of repressive policies of the Communist government. Subsidies were cancelled and the company prohibited from performing in a   hall built for its use. This sparked the creation of an alternative theatre in Roman Catholic churches because the groups had nowhere else to perform. The director of the theatre was quoted as saying, "The only place which is left for us to perform in are the churches." It seems we have come full circle. Rather than the church throwing out the arts, she becomes once again a haven and supporter for the arts!

In June of 1973, Pope Paul VI dedicated a new gallery at the Vatican which houses in some fifty rooms more than 540 individual works of art by 250 well known artists of this century. This was seen as an "overture by the church to the tense, tormented, and often misunderstood artists of our time and their works." In most cases the works were given by the artists or by collectors and were not specifically commissioned works. Excluding works that were intended for places of worship, the works for the gallery were to have a religious reference, intention, or subject. Artists represented in the collection include, among others: Barlach, Baskin, Beekman, Buffet, Chagall, Dali, de Chirico, Gauguin, Klee, Levine, Lipchitz, Manzu, Matisse, Marini, Manessier, Mestrovik, Henry Moore, Nolde, Roualt, Shahn, Sutherland, and Watanabe. Paul VI expressed his hope and wish that from this first survey of modern religious art would spring a new artistic tradition.

For centuries the church was the primary patron of the arts. It is unlikely that we will return to that relationship and it may not be advantageous for the church or artists to do so. Nevertheless, we can take hope that the movement toward bridging the long-time separation between these "close siblings" is surely underway and a most promising sign.

An exhibition at the Museum of Modern Art in 1984 entitled "Primitivism in 20th Century Art: Affinity of the Tribal and the Modern" was sponsored by Philip Morris, Inc. In their full-page advertisement about the exhibit were these words:

> It is a show which sheds new light on and challenges much of our 'received wisdom' about both 'primitive' and 'modern' and their relation to each other. It may be the first art exhibition you've ever seen which asks and answers so many questions about art — and about ourselves.
>
> That's one reason we sponsored this exhibition, and why we urge you to see it...In our business as in yours, *we must constantly ask ourselves new questions*, and be prepared for answers quite different from those we expect. *Sponsorship of art that reminds us of these things is not patronage; it's a business and human necessity*. (emphasis mine)

One can be delighted that a tobacco company was willing to fund such a splendid exhibition and see the importance of it. How much more kinship there is between the church and the arts, and how important it is for us to be willing to ask new questions, to see the arts as part of the church's "business" and a divine/human necessity.

The future of our civilization, its survival and health, is inseparable from the future of its art. Modern art is thus neither a luxury nor a decorative excrescence hanging on the edge of culture. Art is central to any civilization which hopes to remain vital and healthy.

Rollo May

CHAPTER 7

ISSUES OF ESTRANGEMENT

Religion has been on the side of art, even visual art, from the basilica and mosaic of ancient Christianity to the French priests who gave us Audincourt and Ronchamp; and religion has also been the enemy of art from the bishops of Elvira who did not want pictures on the walls of basilicas, to the Vatican bureaucrats who attempted bitterly to prevent the building of Assy near Chamounix.

Samuel Laeuchli

Protestant Christians have always had an appreciative nose for the sweat of ethics; it's any whiff of aesthetics they can't stand.

Theodore Gill

The view that the corporeal is not a fit vehicle for the divine leads to a rejection of music through the ear, pictures through the eye, and sacraments through the mouth.

Roland Bainton

There is evidence of both kinship and estrangement in the relationship of art and faith over time. We have stressed the kinship more than the estrangement, but the conflicts have been there from the beginning and must not be glossed over.

James Wall, editor of *The Christian Century*, asks in an editorial, "What are the factors in modern church life that impede an embrace of the arts, especially the visual kind?" [88] After noting that there was a brief period in the late 1960's when there was excitement about the arts, Wall wonders why today there is still scant attention to the arts in seminary education, religious curriculum, or church life in general. He suggests four reasons:

Utilitarianism A question which constantly lurks in the mind of the clergy is "will it work?" A lack of conviction that involvement with the arts will be useful has dampened the enthusiasm that may have been present at one time. (It could be further suggested that a suspicion of the amount of work it will entail has equally contributed to a lethargic response. Far easier to order from religious house catalog than engage in a give and take with a living, breathing artist!)

The Protestant Work Ethic To many people the arts suggest frivolous pleasure. Involvement with the arts is not considered serious enough, or as contributing to the welfare of humankind ("Those who make art are rarely perceived by others as doing 'real work'" notes Judith Rock.)

A Dichotomy of Spirit and Flesh Religious training is geared primarily to intellect and will rather than the senses and the intuition. But if "life is all of one piece" as Wall affirms, then training in receptivity to the arts can also be training in spirituality, calling us to a "full engagement of spirit with life."

The Question of Authority Traditional sources of authority for faith have been scripture, tradition, and church authority. Are we willing to be open to "hidden meanings" in art forms? Are we ready to risk the uncomfortable possibility that new wisdom and insight may come to us directly through the work of creative artists?

To James Wall's four reasons for the church's failure to incorporate the arts into its program and nurture, can be added two more:

Iconoclasm For many Protestants there is an ambivalence about visual imagery and a residual concern about the prohibition of graven images and idolatry. The roots of iconoclasm – the opposition to religious use of images – are deep and often not fully conscious.

Historically, the acceptance or rejection of images in the church was mixed. The Eastern Orthodox Church considered images vital to worship and church life and never parted from their use. Among Protestant reformers there were interesting differences. "Iconoclastic attitudes and activities were one of the least agreed upon aspects of the Protestant reformation in Germany and Switzerland" writes Margaret Miles. [89] Attention was to be focussed on the "preaching of the word" and nothing should distract from the hearing of the word. Zwingli, though personally attracted to paintings and statues, was against images in the church and insisted they be removed and in many cases destroyed, although stained glass windows could remain. John Calvin warned that images pander to man's desire for a tangible God, yet also wrote that "sculpture and painting are gifts of God. I seek a pure and legitimate use of each." [90] Martin Luther was far more open, writing that, "according to the law of Moses no other images are forbidden than an image of God which one

All three (words, arts, sacrament) are for raising questions and for listening to their echoes in the resonant silence of the Holy; all of them frames for the silence of God as well as for the Word of God. They allow us to listen as well as proclaim.

Judith Rock

It is to be sure better to paint pictures on walls of how God created the world, how Noah built the ark and whatever other good stories there may be, than to paint shameless worldly things. Yes, would to God I could persuade the rich and mighty that they would permit the whole Bible to be painted on houses, on the inside and outside, so that all can see it.

Martin Luther

Artists and theologians alike create the experience of 'Now my eyes are open'. Like the parables of Jesus, they shock us into new perceptions.

Dorothy Lairmore

Art is a frightening, untamed power. Plato knew that; so did Zwingli. It is unpredictable, at times even unexplainable. How rather like the Holy Spirit that would seem!

Nancy Chinn

worships."

Luther poses the question, "If it is not a sin but good to have the image of Christ in my heart, why should it be a sin to have it in my eyes?"

In more recent times we find theologians differing on the use of images. Karl Barth maintained that images and symbols had no place at all in Protestant worship. Paul Tillich, on the other hand, wrote:

> The background of this rejection of the arts of the eye is the fear – and even horror – of a relapse into idolatry… Arts of the eye are more open to idolatrous demonization than the arts of the ear. But the difference is relative, and the very nature of the Spirit stands against the exclusion of the eye from the experience of its presence. [91]

Jesus made eighty-four references to seeing (the eyes, vision, blindness, etc.), sometimes referring to literal physical sight, sometimes to insight. [92] Perhaps they are more related than we normally think. The whole iconoclastic controversy testifies to the power of art and an uneasiness about this power. [93] Art invites direct confrontation and circumvents any effort to control or interpret what the response should be. Margaret Miles calls this "the multi-valence of an image – a range of possible interpretations." [94] There is usually no need for explanation and the work speaks on its own authority.

As artists and religious communities move toward one another, we can expect some ambivalence in this area and should be aware of the need to understand the source of fears that may surface.

Financial Commitment to the Arts. What will it cost? As we begin to build resources, make more attractive places for worship and study, venture to commission visual artists, musicians, or choreographers for new work, there will be those, as in Jesus' day, who will insist that the money should rather be given to the poor. We will do well to remember Jesus' reply:

> Let her alone. Why must you make trouble for her? It is a fine thing she has done for me. You have the poor among you always, and you can help them whenever you like; but you will not always have me. She has done what lay in her power; she is beforehand with anointing my body for burial. I tell you this: wherever in all the world the Gospel is proclaimed, what she has done will be told as her memorial. [95]

The Old Testament offers ample encouragement for the church to give of its substance for art. After the Ten Commandments were given and certain civil and religious laws were set forth, six chapters follow devoted to artistic instructions. Though the Israelites were to be wandering people for a time, their worship was not to be done in a shoddy or casual manner. Their worship was to make use of the finest of materials and the best of their creativity. Robert Plimpton, for ten years Director of Music and Fine Arts at Bryn Mawr Presbyterian Church, has suggested some of the thoughts that might have gone through Moses' mind:

> Come on Lord, I've had enough! Why do you saddle me with these artists? We have just come out of Egypt, we are homeless refugees. How in the world are we going to get all this done? Isn't there an easier way? Can't we just worship you simply and forget about all this art? [96]

But it did not rest on Moses alone, for God said, "See, I have singled out Bezalel son of Uri, son of Hur, of the tribe of Judah.

Even the most liberal of us, who know how hard it is to get donations for even the best of causes, even we are startled and nonplussed by Jesus' pleasure in the spontaneous inefficiency of that Mary who poured her expensive ointments on his unaccustomed feet.

But that is how it is: Jesus at least occasionally responding positively to the irrelevant and unnecessary; or anyway, giving a more spacious definition than we'd expected to both relevance and necessity.

Theodore Gill

[The] corsetting of the human spirit is over...and the church at large doesn't know quite what to make of it yet, but here and there in the parishes there is again the gasp of spontaneity, the stamp and clap and cry of celebration, a whir of wit and even whimsey, a reach for novelty, an attentiveness to the irrelevant but enchanting apes, ivories, and peacocks of God's extravagant creation.

Theodore Gill

Theology and the arts are architectures of meaning, fragile structures through whose doors and windows we glimpse the mystery of our being. Hungry to hear and see some part of the truth about ourselves, we go to church, the synagogue, the theatre. Each time, we hope to be called by name, to be surprised, reminded of who we are and whose we are. The artist and the theologian share the task of inviting us across these mysterious thresholds.

Judith Rock

I have filled him with the spirit of God and endowed him with skill and perception and knowledge for every kind of craft: for the art of designing and working in gold and silver and bronze; for cutting stones to be set, for carving in wood, for every kind of craft." (Exodus 31:1-5) There were talented persons whose gifts were to be used in the worship of God.

Later, when Solomon built the Temple, the scale was even greater for the kingdom had become very prosperous. The Temple art was to include free-standing sculpture, work in bronze and gold, columns with capitals, and needle work. The finest materials and most gifted craftsmen were to be sought to create sacred space for the worship of God.

And so, on down through the centuries the people of God have left a rich heritage of art – from the paintings in the catacombs to the third century murals of the Jewish synagogue at Dura Europus; from the fifth century mosaics of Ravenna to the exquisitely crafted liturgical vessels of the sixth century. Book illuminations, ivory carvings, colorful tapestries, splendid vestments, the magnificent Byzantine, Romanesque, and Gothic cathedrals – all form a priceless heritage which have come down to us. How can we not continue to add to the great witness of the vitality of the Christian faith as expressed through art in our own day?

The debate over how much the church should spend for art is not a new question and may never be put to rest. Yet, as we have shown, the arts can touch religious communities at so many vital places of their life and work – in worship, in ways of teaching and learning, in a ministry of healing and prophetic message to the world it seeks to serve. Surely expenditures of effort and resources are clearly justified and will be amply repaid.

CHAPTER 8

PRACTICAL CONSIDERATIONS

In the light of what has been written, what are some practical ways to live out the concerns and possibilities expressed in this paper? We will look first at some implications for the local church and secondly point to the value of resource agencies which can encourage and facilitate this process in the local church and offer services and programs beyond the capacities of a given local church.

IN THE LOCAL CHURCH

To promote the interest and use of the arts in the local church, forming an arts committee would be a first step. Relating this committee organizationally to the church's worship or education committee would be important both for support and coordination with existing programs. The purpose of such a committee would be to study and implement ways the arts can be used in the church, though any given church may wish to define their purpose more specifically. The kinds of activities and programs which might be considered are suggested in the following pages, which are, of course, by no means exhaustive. Hopefully this list will spark additional ideas as each church lives out its own creative expression and understanding of its message and mission.

The committee will want to educate itself as best it can by reading; study of what other churches have done; and evaluating its own resources, both within the church and the community. It will probably want to narrow its concern to one or two areas in the beginning. Churches concerned primarily with the visual arts would find the book *Visual Art in the Life of the Church* by Richard R. Caemmerer, Jr. a good place to start. Other books relating to educational and theological considerations should

Artists belong in the center of the church, not on the fringe, or as an afterthought or as a "decoration." If we are to create a more humane world, the Kingdom of God, we need the social imagination of artists from every persuasion to tell us the Truth!

Dorothy Lairmore

also be reviewed. (The Bibliography included herein provides a good starting point.) Contact with one's own denominational board and/or one of the resource organizations or institutions listed in these pages would be important as well.

WORSHIP

1. Study the nature of worship. Use books by James White (*Introduction to Christian Worship* or *New Forms of Worship*) to deepen an understanding of the purpose and intent of worship.

2. Study the worship services in your local church. Is the worship service unified? Do the music, sermon, and visual elements work toward a whole, or is it disjointed, even at times working at cross-purposes?

3. Does worship truly serve to bring people into the presence of God; help them in praise or lament? Consider the environment for worship. Does it enhance or detract from these purposes? Is there excitement in the service, or are people put to sleep?

4. Consider how the arts might play a role in enhancing worship. Possibilities include: banners, wall hangings, paraments, altar cloths, dance, dialogue sermons with artists, meditation on an art work, etc. The use of the arts should always be in context and as servant. The use of any art form should not move into the realm of performance when it is being used in the context of worship.

5. Give special attention to changes in the liturgical year. For particular concerns, consider a specially designed "liturgy of indignation" or a "liturgy of celebration," etc.

What churches need to do now to renew self and society is to take spirituality seriously; this means taking art seriously. Not art for the sake of art; not art for the sake of making banners or teapots; not art for sale. But art as prayer, art as meditation.

Matthew Fox

Religion is indeed danced before it is believed. Religious experience begins at the level of symbol, myth, and ritual, rather than signs, concepts or reflective actions...Religion begins with the affections – not intellectual conviction.

John Westerhoff

6. Consider original works of art for the cover of the weekly church bulletin, including children's art. Also, original poetry by members of the congregation could be used.

EDUCATION

1. Offer adult study courses for Sunday morning, weekday evening, or Saturday workshops on such topics as:

   "A Study of the History of Christian Art: From the Catacombs to the Present"

   "Understanding the Liturgical Year: Through Art, Symbol, and Color"

   "Contemporary Artists: Their Perception of Spirit"

   "Art as Meditation/Contemplation"

2. Look at the total educational program of the church to see how much "right-brain" approaches are used as compared to "left brain."

3. With Church School committee or teachers, look at the art which is currently being used, both in teaching (through curriculum material or other sources) as well as pictures which are on the walls of the church school. Where appropriate make suggestions for replacement and purchase of new pictures. Consider prints of masterworks, available at low cost from museums, as well as modest-priced original graphics. If possible, borrow or rent art works so there can be variety and change.

4. Survey other areas of the church – narthex, fellowship hall, parlors, adult classrooms, hallways, sanctuary – con-

Human nature and human society are more deeply motivated by images than by ideas.
Amos Wilder

The meaning of a word is not as exact as the meaning of a color.
Georgia O'Keefe

Seeing comes before words. The child looks and recognizes before it can speak.
John Berger

sider and propose, where appropriate, purchase of quality art, including commissioning original art work for a particular space.

5. Recommend books for the church library which would explore the relation of faith and art as well as art books which can be enjoyed by individuals or used in church school classes. Special purchases might include: *The Gospel in Art by the Peasants of Solentiname*; *The Life of Jesus*, text by Frederich Buechner, photographs by Lee Boltin; *Through the Christian Year: An Illustrated Guide* by Catherine Kapikian; *The Bible and its Painting*; *Aesthetic Dimensions of Religious Education;* etc.

6. Work with the missionaries whom your church supports to provide an exchange between the children of the church schools of drawings and paintings resulting from their Bible studies.

CREATIVITY WITHIN THE CHURCH

1. Find out the talents, hobbies and interests of the members of the congregation. Hold a Congregational Art Show in which members, both old and young, may submit their works of creation. Categories could include: painting, drawing, sculpture, ceramics, pottery, photography, fabric arts, needlepoint, woodwork, calligraphy, poetry, stained glass, macrame, quilting, etc. During the time of the art show (two to four weeks), sermons could deal with creativity as an expression of being made in God's image. People could share during worship services the meaning their creative expression has for them.

2. Various groups could be formed in the church, depending on the number interested:

The image arts always have been and always will be the non-verbal language of the spirit, the silent educator of the soul...The image educates where reason never reaches.

Dorothea Blom

• A craft group which could make altar cloths; wall hangings; a communion chalice; a wooden cross; a needlepoint kneeling bench or chair cushion; or banners for liturgical seasons for use in worship, or to enhance the entrance way, or to celebrate a baptism or wedding. A professional artist could be invited to create any designs from which the group worked.

• A graphics group concerned about effective layouts for church publications, bulletins, logos, and special publicity.

• A photography group which could provide a year-round pictorial record of the activities of the church to be shown at the annual meeting depicting the church at worship, retreat, in various outreach endeavors, in fellowship. Where VCR equipment is available, an even grander visual record could be made. Pictures of new members could be posted, so names and faces could be related.

3. Offer opportunities for people to experience the creative process:

• Find someone qualified to offer a class using the book *Drawing on the Right Side of the Brain* which will introduce people to the ideas as well as the experience of right-brain activity.

• Offer occasions when creative responses are called for. For instance, at a family night or intergenerational evening, give a theme such as "manger, cross, tomb," or "the poor and oppressed," or "world peace." Have people respond in various media. Options could include writing a poem, giving a dramatic skit, mime or clowning, dance, working in clay or wax, making a banner, creating a collage with pictures from magazines and newspapers.

To paint a picture or write a story or compose a song is an incarnational activity. The artist is a servant who is willing to be a birth-giver.

Madeline L'Engle

Gather together to share and celebrate the diversity of gifts and ways of communicating our concerns.

• At a family night have each family create a "family banner" which will show signs and symbols which represent who they are. Others could create a personal banner or a banner which would depict the church's history or credo.

CONTACTS OUTSIDE THE CHURCH

1. Sponsor art shows by professional artists. If suitable space is available, consider having a monthly or quarterly art show. Be sure to arrange for insurance coverage and newspaper publicity. Perhaps the church could make a "purchase award" from the show.

2. Invite artists to share with the church about their art, the creative process, how they see their work. Have them engage in 'dialogue' with the minister in a sermon if appropriate. Invite an artist to be "in residence" – providing space for them to work and an opportunity for people to see the creative process at work – an excellent use for any unused rooms which may have resulted from declining Sunday School enrollments!

3. Organize a tour of artists' studios to see the artist at work in his/her own space.

4. If the church is in an area where many artists live or go to school, offer opportunities for them to gather to share interests and concerns.

5. Sponsor a tour of the local museum. Request a special guide for a custom-made tour which will view art from various perspectives, such as "Treasures of Christian Art" or "Understanding Modern Art." Visit local galleries when

It's empowering to the creative act to be nurtured, to be loved, to be respected and to be in a community where the issues that are germane to the church are forever on everyone's lips. Being in this kind of community has a direct relationship to the work produced (by the artist.)

Catherine Kapikian

there are shows of special interest.

6.   Have a tour of churches known for their impressive architecture or significant works of art.

7.   Form a group which will together attend current movies or theater with opportunity provided for discussion afterwards. With the use of a VCR, a series of movies at the church could be shown and discussed – a "Sunday Night at the Movies" or "Friday Flicks."

PROPHETIC OUTREACH

1.   Consider the various ways in which the arts can bring the concerns of the world to the attention of the congregation: it may be a visual portrayal by film, slide, or picture of the plight of an Ethiopian child or a South African family, or a projection of a slide of Picasso's *Guernica* to bring to consciousness the horrors of war.

2.   Encourage members to take part in "Banners for Peace" and have them presented at church.

3.   Be aware of resources in the community such as "Artists Call," a group of artists devoted to dealing with social issues. Offer to display photographs taken by journalists in Central America.

4.   Broaden understanding of other races and cultures by inviting Cambodian children to share their native dances, or hosting a show of art works by inner-city children.

5.   Consider taking art and/or music to prisons, nursing and retirement homes, hospitals – both for enjoyment and for the making.

My art is expressed in hard wood or stone. It is outside time and space. Art is a song and a prayer at the same time...We must be in love with eternity so that our works are at least a shadow of it.

Ivan Mestrovic

No significant vision can find full expression within the confines of private life. Sooner or later, if it is to be fulfilled, it must find an outlet in the public realm. It may be an idea, a book, a work of art, a social movement or program. Impulses such as these, however private their origins, seek public expression as a plant seeks light – and for much the same reason: to be nurtured into growth...A work of art needs to be seen and enriched by the viewer before it comes to fruition...without public experience we cannot experience the fullness of God's word for our lives.

Parker Palmer

6. Form a group for mime or clowning that can "take to the streets" in downtown areas or shopping malls.

7. Study ways the church can reach outside its own walls to connect with public life. A study of Parker Palmer's book *The Company of Strangers* would be most helpful in this regard.

A PLACE OR AGENCY AVAILABLE FOR RESOURCING THE LOCAL CHURCH IN THIS 'ART MINISTRY'

Because most local churches will be limited in their resources, certain agencies or organizations devoted specifically to helping local churches explore the possibilities in the arts are needed. Whether this is provided by a Parish Resource Center, a Presbytery Office, a Seminary, or any other specific organization, the following services could be provided:

1. Workshops and Seminars on some of the issues outlined in this paper.

    Secure well-qualified persons who can address these concerns, including:

    The Place of Visual Arts or Drama,
        and Dance in the Church
    Theology and the Arts
    Art as Meditation/Contemplation
    How to Plan a Religious Arts Festival
    Creating Dynamic Environments for Worship
    Our Heritage in Christian Art
    Religion and Art in Conflict/Concert
    Christian Symbolism and Iconography
    The Nature of Creativity: Its Theory and Practice

We often speak of 'gathering' our thoughts. These images of the Christ, gathered as one gathers flowers to make a bouquet, with no other thought than the love of beauty itself, may help to focus our thoughts upon that vital point where shapes and colours set us musing.

Marcelle Auclair

Art and Social Justice (panel of artists)
Contemporary Artists and their Perceptions of Spirit
What Are the Questions Modern Art is Asking?
A History of Worship
Music, Arts, and Movement in Worship
A Study of Hymnody – Old and New

These workshops could be offered at local churches, or district-wide events, summer schools, continuing education events for lay and clergy at seminaries, etc.

2. Maintain resources for churches in terms of books, slides, art reproductions, original graphics, films, etc., available for borrowing, rental, or purchase.

3. Keep a scrapbook of events and programs sponsored by local churches to provide inspiration and networking.

4. Publish a quarterly newsletter which will provide substantive articles, book reviews, resources in film and television, listing of area conferences and workshops. This could contain original poetry and art work and be designed by graphic artists.

5. Encourage churches to find artists in their own local churches. Find them in the community. Establish a roster of artists who are open to do commissions for churches. Provide guidelines for churches who wish to commission original work.

6. Provide an opportunity for artists to get together to share their own concerns.

7. Explore ways of challenging artists to address certain themes.

Because the one who by excellency of nature transcends all quantity and size and magnitude, who has his being in the form of God, has now, by taking upon himself the form of a slave, contracted himself into a quantity and size and has acquired a physical identity, do not hesitate any longer to draw pictures and to set forth, for all to see, him who has chosen to let himself be seen.

John of Damascus

8. Maintain a listing of resource persons in all the arts including dance, clowning, drama, puppetry, etc. Have video tapes available where appropriate.

9. Maintain an ongoing gallery of art work by contemporary artists. Make this show available for travel to local churches. Where possible, have the artists present for the opening of the show. Exhibits could include original art work as well as fine reproductions (not necessarily in the same show.) Art shows could focus on special issues or themes such as Lent, Advent, Devotional Art, Liturgical Art, Art as Prophetic Message, Christian Art from Other Cultures, etc..

CHAPTER 9

CHALLENGE AND HOPE

After such a long separation, as art and faith discover anew their sense of kinship, there will be no easy resolutions. We need those who will lead us in experiments in reconnection between the arts and faith. Some risk taking will be required which may cause ripples if not waves in congregations and seminaries. We can be grateful for the current high interest in the arts in the culture at large, which gives the church a unique opportunity to re-establish her historic roots with the arts.

The very cataclysmic nature of our times should override any remaining uneasiness or residual suspicion which exists between these close siblings. Beyond any narrow limitation of concern, whether of religion or art, we must join energies and vision so that new life can be released to a spiritually hungry world.

The mandala of modern art, in all its vast diversity, unfolds around a mysterious center, which as chaos and blackness, as numinosum and as change, is pregnant with a new doom, but also with a new world...Our time and our destiny and often our art as well, strikes us in the face, perhaps also in order to fling us into the void of the center which is the center of transformation and birth...

For despite all the despair and darkness which are still more evident in us and our art than the secret forces of the new birth and the new synthesis, we must not forget that no epoch, amid the greatest danger to its existence, has shown so much readiness to burst the narrow limits of its horizon and open itself to the great power which is striving to rise out of the unknown, here and everywhere in the world.

Erich Neumann

FOOTNOTES

1. Theodore Gill, lecture at Seminar on "Theology and the Arts" at Princeton Theological Seminary, November, 1984.

2. Ibid.

3. Abraham Joshua Heschel, *Quest for God* (New York, Crossroad,1982), p. 118.

4. This is an obvious oversimplification of a complex history. For further clarification about the differences in the church's response to art through the centuries, in both the Eastern and Western Church, see the following: Jane Dillenberger, *Style and Content in Christian Art;* Emile Male, *Religious Art from Twelfth to Eighteenth Century;* Margaret Miles, *Image as Insight; Visual Understanding in Western Christianity and Secular Culture;* and C. R. Morey, *Christian Art.*

5. Langdon B. Gilkey, "Can Art Fill the Vacuum?," *Art, Creativity and the Sacred,* edited by Diane Apostolos-Cappadona (New York, Crossroad, 1984), p. 188.

6. John Westerhoff, III, "What Has Zion to Do with Bohemia?," *Religious Education,* January-February 1981, p. 15.

7. "In California a Boom in Art Museums," *Philadelphia Inquirer*, 16-I, May 25, 1986.

8. Jacques Barzun, *The Use and Abuse of Art* (A. W. Mellon Lectures, 1973, Princeton University Press, 1947), p. 30.

9. Ibid.

10. Paul Tillich, *Theology of Culture* (New York, Oxford University Press, 1959).

11. Jane and John Dillenberger, *Perceptions of the Spirit in Twentieth Century American Art* (Indianapolis Museum of Art, 1977).

12. Mircea Eliade, "The Sacred and the Modern Artist," *Art, Creativity and the Sacred*, p. 180.

13. M. C. Escher, *The Infinite World of M. C. Escher* (New York, Abradale Press, Harry Abrams, Inc., 1984), p. 15.

14. Erich Neumann, *Art and the Creative Unconscious* (Bollingen Series LXI, Princeton University Press, 1959), p. 127.

15. Dorothy Sayers, as quoted in *Art in Action – Toward a Christian Aesthetic*, by Nicholas Wolterstorff (Grand Rapids, Michigan, William Eerdman Publishing Co., 1980), p. ix.

16. Walter L. Nathan, *Art and the Message of the Church* (Philadelphia, Westminster Press, 1961), p. 189.

17. Victoria Donohue, *Exhibition of Liturgical Arts*, 41st International Eucharistic Congress, July, 1976, "Introduction," p. 14.

18. Marshall McLuhan, as quoted in James F. White, *New Forms of Worship* (Nashville, Abingdon, 1971), p. 31.

19. Aiden Nichols, *The Art of God Incarnate – Theology and Symbol from Genesis to the Twentieth Century* (New York, Paulist Press, 1980), p. 7.

20. *Applause*, February, 1985. Magazine of WHYY TV12. RJR Associates, Inc., Bala Plaza, Bala Cynwyd, Pennsylvania.

21. White, ibid.

22. Ibid., p. 48.

23. John H. Westerhoff, III, and John D. Eusden, *The Spiritual Life: Learning East and West* (New York, Seabury Press, 1982), p. 41.

24. Erwin R. Goodenoughe, *Psychology of Religious Experience* (New York, Basic Books, Inc. Publisher, 1965), p. 183.

25. Annie Dillard, *Teaching a Stone to Talk* (New York, Harper & Row, 1982), p. 69-70.

26. Thomas Merton, as quoted in *The Choice Is Always Ours*, edited by Dorothy B. Phillips and Elizabeth Boyden Howes (Wheaton, Illinois, The Theosophical Publishing House, 1948), pp. 351-352.

27. Nathan, idem, p. 123.

28. Richard R. Caemmerer, Jr., *Visual Art in the Life of the Church* (Minneapolis, Augsburg Publishing House, 1983), p. 91.

29. Nathan, p. 120.

30. As quoted in *Genesis,* Fall/Winter, 1982, Center for Faith and Arts, Saverna Park, Maryland, p. 3.

31. "Rebirth of a Mountain Parish" by James Dodson. Country Journal Publishing Co., December, 1983.

32. Bartlett was the cover artist for the September, 1986 issue of *American Artist*, in which "Festival of Shelter" is reproduced.

33. John W. Dixon, Jr., *Art and the Theological Imagination* (New York, Seabury Press, 1978), p. 61.

34. Betty Edwards, *Drawing on the Right Side of the Brain* (J. P. Tarcher, Inc., St. Martin's Press, New York, 1979), p. 36.

35. Maria Harris, "A Model for Aesthetic Education," *Aesthetic Dimensions of Religious Education*, p. 145

36. Published by *Christian Education: Shared Approaches*, in 1984.

37. Sara Little, *To Set One's Heart – Belief and Teaching in the Church* (Atlanta, John Knox Press, 1983), p. 63.

38. Lawrence Gowing, *The Bible and Its Painters* (New York, Macmillan Company, 1983), p. 11.

39. American Library Color Slide Co., P. O.Box 5810, Grand Central Station, New York, NY, 10017.

40. John Cook, "Sources for the Study of Christianity and the Arts," *Art, Creativity and the Sacred,* pp. 321-329.

41. Margaret Miles, *Image as Insight:Visual Understanding in Western Christianity and Secular Culture* (Boston, Beacon Press, 1985).

42. *The Gospel in Art by the Peasants of Solentiname* (New York, Mary Knoll, 1984), p. 5.

43. Elisabeth Moltmann-Wendel, *The Women Around Jesus* (New York, Crossroad, 1982).

44. Hans-Ruedi Weber, *Experiments with Bible Study* (Philadelphia, Westminister Press, 1981), p. 28.

45. Margaret Miles, idem, p. 65.

46. Pierre Teilhard de Chardin, *Hymn of the Universe* (New York, Harper and Row, 1965), p. 41ff.

47. Dorothea Blom, *Encounters with Art* (Pendle Hill Pamphlet, 1963), p. 5.

48. As quoted by Nichols, *Idem,* p. 101.

49. Little, idem, p. 68.

50. *Meditations with Hildegard of Bingen* (Santa Fe, New Mexico, Bear and Company, 1982), p. 86.

51. Matthew Fox, *Breakthrough: Meister Eckhart's Creation Spirituality in New Translation* (Garden City, New York, Doubleday, 1977), pp. 404-407.

52. Carl Jung, *Psyche and Symbol* (Garden City, New York, Doubleday Anchor Books, 1958), p. 314.

53. Matthew Fox, *Original Blessing* (Santa Fe, New Mexico, Bear and Company, 1983), p. 195.

54. Matthew Fox, "Art, Spirituality and Social Justice," tape cassette, (Santa Fe, New Mexico, Bear and Company).

55. Paul Tillich, "Existential Aspects of Modern Art," *The Arts in Communication of Faith*, p. 38.

56. Carl Jung, *Man and His Symbols* (New York, Dell, 1964), p. 84.

57. Tillich, *Theology of Culture*, p. 58.

58. Jung, ibid., p. 90.

59. Diane Apostolos-Cappadona, "Reflections on Art and the Spirit: A Conversation," *Art, Creativity, and the Sacred*, p. 28.

60. Tillich, ibid., p. 58.

61. T. S. Eliot, "The Waste Land," in *T. S. Eliot, The Complete Poems and Plays 1909-1950* (New York, Harcourt Brace, 1971), p. 38.

62. Jung, "Commentary on the Secret of the Golden Flower," *Psyche and Symbol*, p. 313.

63. Ira Progoff, *The Symbolic and the Real* (McGraw-Hill Book Company, 1963), p. 220.

64. Gerald H. Slusser, "Language and Symbols in the Human Psyche," *Aesthetic Dimensions of Religious Education*, p. 217.

65. Walter Brueggemann, *The Prophetic Imagination* (Philadelphia, Fortress Press, 1978), p. 50.

66. Ibid., p. 51.

67. Ibid., p. 45.

68. Ibid.

69. Denise Levertov, as quoted in the article "A Leading Poet's Plea for the Imagination," *Philadelphia Inquirer*, Nov. 19, 1984.

70. Rollo May, *The Courage to Create* (New York, W. W. Norton and Company, 1975), p. 35.

71. Fox, *Original Blessing*, p. 193.

72. Andre Malraux, *The Voices of Silence* (Frogmore, St. Albans, Herts., Paladan, 1974).

73. Tillich, *Theology of Culture*, p. 58.

74. Barzun, idem, p. 149.

75. *Image Breaking/Image Building*, Linda Clark, Marian Ronan and Eleanor Walker, eds. (New York, Pilgrim Press, 1981), p. 2.

76. Father John Miller, *Exhibition of Liturgical Arts*, Forty-first International Eucharistic Congress, 1976, p. 22.

77. Roger Ortmayer, "The Graphic Arts: Painting," *The Arts in Communication of Faith*, p. 83.

78. Ronald Goetz, "Art in Seminary: Revolutionizing Theological Education," *Christian Century Magazine*, March 19-26, 1986.

79. Rainer Maria Rilke, *Rodin* (Salt Lake City, Peregrine Smith, Inc., 1979), p. 11.

80. Neumann, *Art and the Creative Unconscious,* p. 129.

81. Matthew Fox, *A Spirituality Named Compassion* (Minneapolis, Minn., Winston Press, 1979), pp. 117-124.

82. Langdon Gilkey, *Idem,* p.191.

83. Lewis Hyde, "The Commerce of the Creative Spirit," *The American Poetry Review*, March/April, 1983, p. 7.

84. May Sarton, as quoted by Hyde, op. cit., p. 8.

85. *Philadelphia Inquirer*, September 5, 1986.

86. *Philadelphia Inquirer*, April 23, 1983.

87. *Philadelphia Inquirer*, October 1984.

88. *The Christian Century*, June, 1986.

89. Miles, *Image as Insight,* p. 104.

90. John Calvin, as quoted in Albert Moore's *Iconography of Religions: An Introduction* (Philadelphia, Fortress Press, 1977), p. 272.

91. Tillich, *Systematic Theology*, Volume III, p. 200.

92. Father Giles Le Vasseur, OSB, in lecture on "Art and Spirituality" at Paul VI Institute for the Arts, Washington, DC, November 8, 1986.

93. See Nancy Chinn, "The Iconoclastic Controversy in New Clothes" in *Let The People Worship* (Schuyler Creative Arts Institute), Volume 2 Issue 2 (Spring, 1987).

94. Miles, idem, p. 30.

95. Mark 14:6-9.

96. Robert Plimpton, "The New Song of the New Covenant," address to Women's Association Luncheon, March 1978, Bryn Mawr Presbyterian Church, p. 4.

AFFIRMATION OF THE ARTS

Whereas, we are heirs of the Biblical inheritance of art, of the God who created from out of chaos and who put life and breath into the dust of the earth, of David who danced before the ark and sang songs of faith, of Miriam who sang songs of joy, of Jesus who drew pictures in parables and raised the common elements of our lives to a symbolic and sacred use, and of John who revealed a new vision of heaven coming to earth;

Whereas, the Church through the ages has been a patron and preserver of the arts and the artists;

Whereas, the United Church of Christ firmly believes in the development of the whole person as a cultural, social and political being;

Whereas, the potential for magnificent creative activity exists within and among each of us;

Whereas, we believe that the arts are a prophetic and effective channel for the mediation of God's judgement and grace for the redemption of the world; we are drawn into a work of art, we experience its transforming power; the arts open us to new ways of understanding both personal and public life and give us insight and energy to act in love and justice for the sake of the Holy.

RESOLVED, That the 11th General Synod of the United Church of Christ affirms the contribution of arts and artists that enrich the quality and the vitality of life in our Church and world. We recognize that artists illuminate the symbols by which the religious dimensions of life and experience are made known. Also, that they enable the people of God to experience and express the living and liberating power of God, and to renew, sustain, and transform people in a new sense of themselves as persons and in relation to each other in community;

RESOLVED, That we encourage freedom to bring to creative expression the religious dimension of our life which nurtures community;

RESOLVED, That we urge the United Church of Christ, through its instrumentalities, publications and church-related institutions (educational, welfare, health, etc.) to recognize further and support the arts:

RESOLVED, That we urge local churches to:

1. Encourage the expression of all forms of art.

2. Examine their use of physical space in order to consider sharing space available with the community's artists.

3. Support and expand the number of artists in residence both in the Church and in the community.

4. Struggle for justice for the artists in our society.

5. Support arts agencies and councils, municipal governments, and school districts, at state and local levels, to the end that no one be denied opportunities to create and experience art, because of barriers, e.g., circumstance, class, race, sex, income, or remoteness;

RESOLVED, That we encourage all members of the Church, laity and clergy, to open themselves to the power and dynamics of the contemporary arts.

We encourage seminaries and colleges related to the Church to take seriously aesthetic ways of knowing and communicating through art the judgement and grace of God in their curricula and degree programs. We encourage the judicatories of the Church to recognize and support certain churches as having special ministries to and with artists. We support and urge membership in the United Church of Christ Fellowship in the Arts.

Adopted by the 11th General Synod
of the United Church of Christ
July, 1977
Washington, D.C.

HOW YOUR CHURCH CAN COMMISSION ORIGINAL ART

Why commission original art? Because original art enriches worship and great art takes people to new places. Original work can be an affordable alternative to catalogue art.

Once your church decides to commission a piece, you should be prepared to spend a lot of time in the initial process of selecting an artist. Establishing good dialogue and developing trust are the most important steps in dealing with an artist. Whether the artist is well-known or unestablished, the process is the same.

If your church does not have a particular artist in mind from the beginning, set up a committee and invite artists to a meeting to present work they have done. If you are still undecided about several contenders, ask each one to make a clear presentation of what the finished work will look like. This is called a design concept, and you will have to pay each artist to prepare one.

Once you select the artist, your minister should write a lettter of confirmation to acknowledge the commission. The commission is a significant step. Whether or not you draw up a contract is a matter of individual preference.

Interfering with the creative process – adding a new design element, changing a color – is a point at which many committees founder. Once you have chosen the artist, your committee must not interfere. Otherwise you will destroy the integrity of the finished work.

If the commission is very large, you may want to divide it into two phases to protect your church from sponsoring a finished product which doesn't meet your expectations. Phase one is design. The artist presents a scale model and full color renderings of the finished work. You may expect to pay half of the cost of the project at this point.

Phase two is executing the design. If supplies are expensive, the artist may ask you to pay for them in advance. Otherwise you pay upon completion. Once the commission is finished, your church may wish to celebrate the new addition to its worship life with a ceremony acknowledging the artist and the work.

by Catherine Kapikian
Artist-in-Residence
Wesley Theological Seminary

BIBLIOGRAPHY

ART AND THE BIBLE

Bernard, Bruce. *The Bible and its Painters*. London: Orbis Publications, Ltd., 1983.

Blom, Dorothea. *Art Responds to the Bible*. Pendle Hill Pamphlet, 1974.

Coen, Rena Neumann. *The Old Testament in Art*. Minneapolis, Minnesota (Fine Art Books for Young People), Lerner Publications Co., 1970.

Harby, Clifton, ed. *The Bible in Art, Twenty Centuries of Famous Bible Paintings*. New York: Covici, Friede, Inc., 1936.

Mayor, A. Hyatt. *Rembrandt and the Bible.* New York: Metropolitan Museum of Art, 1979.

Satinsky, Robin, editor. *Bible and Art, 12th Century – 20th Century*. Villanova, Pennsylvania: Donglumur Foundation, 1976.

Schaeffer, Francis A. *Art and the Bible.* Downers Grove, Illinois: Intervarsity Press, 1973.

Scharper, ed. *The Gospel in Art by the Peasants of Solentiname*. Mary Knoll, New York: Orbis Publisher, 1984.

Shissler, Barbara Johnson. *The New Testament in Art*. Minneapolis, Minnesota: (Fine Arts Books for Young People), Lerner Publications, 1970.

Thomas, Denis. *The Face of Christ.* New York: Doubleday, 1979.

Weber, Hans-Ruedi. *Experiments with Bible Study.* Philadelphia: Westminster Press, 1981.

—————————, *Immanuel: The Coming of Jesus in Art and the Bible.* Grand Rapids, Michigan: William B. Eerdmans, 1984.

ART AND RELIGIOUS EDUCATION

Durka, Gloria, and Joanmarie Smith, eds. *Aesthetic Dimensions of Religious Education.* New York: Paulist Press, 1979.

Kapikian, Catherine A. *Through the Christian Year: An Illustrated Guide.* Nashville: Abingdon Press, 1983.

Little, Sara. *To Set One's Heart – Belief and Teaching in the Church.* Atlanta: John Knox Press, 1983.

Medkeff-Rose, Brian. *The Play's the Thing.* Nashville: Abingdon Press, 1986.

Nathan, Walter L. *Art and the Message of the Church.* Philadelphia: Westminster Press, 1961.

Sill, Gertrude Grace. *A Handbook of Symbols in Christian Art.* New York: Collier Books, Macmillan Publishing Co., 1975.

Tobey, Kathrene M. *Learning and Teaching Through the Senses.* Philadelphia: Westminster Press, 1970.

Ward, Wendy. *Gift of God – Gift to God: Living the Word through Artistry.* Geneva Press, 1984 (Youth Elective Course, CE:SA)

ART AND WORSHIP

Creator Magazine. Dublin, Ohio: Church Music Associates.

Let The People Worship. San Carlos, California: Schuyler Institute for Worship and the Arts.

Modern Liturgy Magazine. San Jose, California: Resource Publications.

White, James F. *New Forms of Worship.* Nashville: Abingdon Press, 1971.

——————, *Introduction to Christian Worship.* Nashville: Abingdon Press, 1980.

Wolfe, Betty. *The Banner Book.* Wilton, Connecticut: Morehouse-Barlow Co., Inc., 1974.

THE VISUAL ARTS

Arnheim, Rudolf. *Art and Visual Perception: A Psychology of the Creative Eye.* Berkeley: University of California Press, 1954.

Blom, Dorothea. *Encounters with Art.* Pendle Hill Pamphlet, 1963.

——————, *Life Journey of a Quaker Artist*. Pendle Hill
Pamphlet, 1980.

The Borgia Apartment and Contemporary Art in the Vatican
(complete catalog). Musei e Gallerie Pontificie, 1974.

Caemmerer, Richard R., Jr. *Visual Art in the Life of the Church*.
Minneapolis: Augsburg Publishing House, 1983.

Davies, Horton and Hugh. *Sacred Art in a Secular Century*.
Collegeville, Minnesota: The Liturgical Press, 1978.

Dillenberger, Jane and John. *Perceptions of the Spirit in
Twentieth Century American Art*. Indianapolis Museum of Art,
1977.

Edwards, Betty. *Drawing on the Right Side of the Brain*. Los
Angeles: J. P. Tarcher, Inc., St. Martin's Press, New York,
1979.

Escher, M. C. *The Infinite World of M. C. Escher*. New York:
Abradale Press, Harry Abrams, Inc., 1984.

Exhibition of Liturgical Arts, Forty-first International Eucharistic
Congress, 1976.

Getlein, Frank and Dorothy. *Christianity in Modern Art*. Milwau-
kee: Bruce Publishing Co., 1961.

Judson, Sylvia Shaw. *The Quiet Eye – A Way of Looking at
Pictures*. Chicago: Regnery Gateway, Inc., 1954.

Morey, C. R. *Christian Art*. New York: W. W. Norton and Company, 1958.

Ouspensky, Leonid, and Vladimir Lossky. *The Meaning of Icons.* Crestwood, New York: St. Vladimir Seminary Press, 1983.

Piper, David. *Looking at Art.* New York: Random House, 1984.

THEOLOGICAL AND PSYCHOLOGICAL STUDIES

Apostolos-Cappadona, Diane, editor. *Art, Creativity and the Sacred.* New York: Crossroad, 1984.

The Arts in Communication of Faith. Nashville: United Methodist Church, Graded Press, 1969.

Barzun, Jacques. *The Use and Abuse of Art* (A. W. Mellon Lectures, 1973). Princeton: Princeton University Press, 1974.

Berdyaev, Nicolas. *The Meaning of the Creative Act.* New York: Collier Books, 1962.

Brueggemann, Walter. *The Prophetic Imagination.* Philadelphia: Fortress Press, 1978.

Clark, Ronan, and Walter, eds. *Image Breaking/Image Building.* New York: Pilgrim Press, 1981.

Dillard, Annie. *Teaching a Stone to Talk.* New York: Harper and Row, 1982.

Dillenberger, Jane. *Style and Content in Christian Art: from the Catacombs to the Chapel Designed by Matisse a Vence, France.* New York: Crossroad Publishing Company, 1986.

Dillenberger, John. *A Theology of Artistic Sensibilities – the Visual Arts and the Church*. New York: Crossroad Publishing Company, 1986.

Dixon, John W., Jr. *Art and the Theological Imagination*. New York: Seabury Press, 1978.

Edinger, Edward. *Ego and Archetype*. New York: Penguin Books, 1972.

Eichenberg, Fritz. *Art and Faith*. Pendle Hill Pamphlet 68, 1952.

Fox, Matthew. *Breakthrough: Meister Eckhart's Creation Spirituality in New Translation*. Garden City, New York: Doubleday, 1977.

—————, *Original Blessing*. Santa Fe, New Mexico: Bear and Company, 1983.

—————, *A Spirituality Named Compassion*. Minneapolis, Minnesota: Winston Press, 1979.

—————, "Art, Spirituality and Social Justice," Tape Cassette. Santa Fe, New Mexico: Bear and Company, n.d.

Goodenoughe, Erwin Ramsdell. *The Psychology of Religious Experience*. New York: Basic Books, Inc., 1965.

Grabar, Andre. *Christian Iconography, a Study of Its Origins*. Princeton University Press, 1968.

Henri, Robert. *The Art Spirit*. Compiled by Margery Ryerson. New York: Lippincott, 1960.

Jung, Carl G. *Man and His Symbols*. New York: Dell Publishing Company, 1964.

————, *Modern Man in Search of a Soul*. ·New York: Harcourt, Brace and World, 1933.

————, *Psyche and Symbol*. Garden City, New York: Doubleday Anchor Books, 1958.

Kandinsky, Wassily. *Concerning the Spiritual in Art*. New York: Dover Publications, Inc., 1977.

Kung, Hans. *Art and the Question of Meaning*. New York: Crossroad, 1981.

Kunkel, Fritz. *Creation Continues*. Waco, Texas: Word Books, 1973.

Laeuchli, Samuel. *Religion and Art in Conflict*. Philadelphia: Fortress Press, 1980.

L'Engle, Madeleine. *Walking on Water: Reflections on Faith and Art*. Wheaton, Illinois: Harold Shaw, 1980.

Malraux, Andre. *The Voices of Silence*. Frogmore, St. Albans, Herts.: Paladan, 1974.

May, Rollo. *The Courage to Create*. New York: W. W. Norton and Co., 1975.

Miles, Margaret. *Image as Insight: Visual Understanding in Western Christianity and Secular Culture*. Boston, Massachusetts: Beacon Press, 1985.

Moore, Albert. *Iconography of Religions: An Introduction*. Philadelphia: Fortress Press, 1977.

Neumann, Erich. *Art and the Creative Unconscious* (Bollingen Series LXI). Princeton: Princeton University Press, 1959.

Nichols, Aiden. *The Art of God Incarnate – Theology and Symbol from Genesis to the Twentieth Century.* New York: Paulist Press, 1980.

Otto, Rudolf. *The Idea of the Holy.* London: Oxford University Press, 1958.

Palmer, Parker. *The Company of Strangers.* New York: Crossroad, 1981.

Pelikan, Jaroslav. *Jesus Through the Centuries.* New Haven: Yale University Press, 1985.

Progoff, Ira. *The Symbolic and the Real.* New York: McGraw-Hill Book Company, 1963.

Purdy, William. *Seeing and Believing – Theology and Art.* Butler, Wisconsin: Clergy Book Service, 1976.

Rank, Otto. *Art and Artist.* New York: Alfred A. Knopf, Inc., 1932.

Richards, M. C. *The Crossing Point.* Middletown, Connecticut: Wesleyan University Press, 1986.

——————, *Centering.* Middletown, Connecticut: Wesleyan University Press, 1962.

Robbins, Lois B. *Waking Up in the Age of Creativity.* Santa Fe, New Mexico: Bear and Co., 1984.

Rookmaaker, H. R. *Modern Art and the Death of a Culture.* Leicester, England: Inter-Varsity Press, 1970.

A Thomas Merton Reader, Ed. Thomas P. McDonnell. New York: Image Books, 1974.

Tillich, Paul. *Systematic Theology*, Volume III. Chicago: University of Chicago Press, 1963.

—————, *Theology of Culture.* New York: Oxford University Press, 1959.

Westerhoff, John H., III, and John D. Eusden. *The Spiritual Life: Learning East and West.* New York: Seabury Press, 1982.

Wolterstorff, Nicholas. *Art in Action – Toward a Christian Aesthetic.* Grand Rapids, Michigan: William Eerdman Publishing Company, 1980.

Malé, Emile. *Art and Artists of the Middle Ages.* Redding Ridge, Connecticut: Black Swans Books, Ltd., 1986.

—————, *Religious Art from the 12th to the 18th Century.* Princeton University Press, 1949.

OTHER RESOURCES

American Library Color Slide Company, Inc.
P. O. Box 5810, Grand Central Station
New York, NY 10017

ARC
The Society for the Arts, Religion and
    Contemporary Culture, Inc.
619 Lexington Avenue
New York, NY 10022

> *regarding membership information for the above:*
> c/o Robin Pearse
> Studio on the Canal
> Princeton, NJ 08540

Center for the Arts and Religion
Catherine Kapikian, Director
Wesley Theological Seminary
4500 Massachusetts Ave., N. W.
Washington, DC 20016

Christians in the Visual Arts
P. O. Box 10247
Arlington, VA 22210

Interfaith Forum on Religion, Art and Architecture
1777 Church Street, N. W.
Washington, DC 20036

Institute in Culture and Creation Spirituality
3500 Mountain Blvd.
Oakland, CA 94619

Pacific School of Religion
1798 Scenic Ave.
Berkeley, CA 94709

Paul VI Institute for the Arts
924 G Street, N. W.
Washington, DC 20001

Potters House Press
P. O. Box 21039
Washington, DC 20009
a quarterly publication which promotes the powerful bond between faith and art. $12 for four issues.

Sacred Dance Guild
P.O. Box 177
Peterborough, NH 03458

Schuyler Institute For Worship And The Arts
2757 Melendy Drive, Suite 15
San Carlos, CA 94070

The Fellowship of United Methodists in Worship, Music and the other Arts
159 Ralph McGill Blvd. NE
Room 501C
Atlanta, GA 30308

The Sharing Company
P.O. Box 2224
Austin, TX 78767

United Church of Christ Fellowship in the Arts
Lorraine Vagner, Membership Chair
9915 S. W. 74th Street
Miami, FL 33173